Welcome

Welcome to this book on communication, where I share a model I created called the 'IMPACT' model, and where I share many of the lessons and tips I've learned over my 30 years as a human resource professional.

Since writing the book I've been humbled by the positive reaction and by the kind words on how the model and the tips have helped overcome the challenges we all face as we communicate to our workforce (not an easy audience!). One lovely HR manager posted on social media that this was her "go to" book which she uses each time she does a communication campaign. I'm so pleased by this, for this was my intent, wanting to help others avoid the mistakes I've made, and follow the steps that myself and industry leaders have suggested.

I so enjoyed writing this book that I co-wrote another one, titled *Build it: A rebel playbook for world-class employee engagement*, partnering with Glenn Elliott, Founder of Reward Gateway. If you'd like to learn more about this book or anything related to employee engagement, of which communication is a critical part, you can go to www.rebelplaybook.com.

To end, let me say that I'm beginning to work on my next book, which combines the ideas of the first two by writing a rebel playbook relating specifically to communication using the IMPACT model. Just like *Build it*, it will contain lots of 'plays' or stories of what rebels are doing, so if you're a communications rebel please do get in touch with me by emailing debra@rebelplaybook.com. I'd love to chat about how you can be a part of the book!

All the best to you as you create and deliver your communications. I hope that it helps you deliver it with IMPACT, meeting the needs of you and your business!

All the best,

Debra

Effective HR Communication

A framework for communicating HR programmes with IMPACT

Debra Corey

LONDON PHILADELPHIA NEW DELHI

Publisher's note

Every possible effort has been made to ensure that the information contained in this book is accurate at the time of going to press, and the publishers and author cannot accept responsibility for any errors or omissions, however caused. No responsibility for loss or damage occasioned to any person acting, or refraining from action, as a result of the material in this publication can be accepted by the editor, the publisher or the author.

First published in Great Britain and the United States in 2016 by Kogan Page Limited

2nd Floor, 45 Gee Street
London
EC1V 3RS
United Kingdom

1518 Walnut Street, Suite 1100
Philadelphia PA 19102
USA

4737/23 Ansari Road
Daryaganj
New Delhi 110002
India

ISBN 978 0 7494 7616 8
E-ISBN 978 0 7494 7619 9

British Library Cataloguing-in-Publication Data

A CIP record for this book is available from the British Library.

Library of Congress Control Number

2016932637

Typeset by Graphicraft Limited, Hong Kong
Print production managed by Jellyfish
Printed and bound by Ashford Colour Press Ltd.

CONTENTS

LIST OF FIGURES

LIST OF TABLES

For my husband Ken and my children Chloe and Anthony, my father Herb and sister Lauren, who encouraged and supported me in writing my first (and hopefully not last) book. Also, to my mother (aka proofreader) and brother (aka inspiration), who had a huge impact on my desire and drive to write this book. Finally, to all of those that contributed to the book, I really appreciate your help.

Introduction

In today's competitive environment where we are doing everything we can to compete for talent, effective communication ensures we are showcasing our HR programmes in a way which will help us attract, retain and engage our key talent. Whether introducing new HR programmes or relaunching existing ones, communications help us deliver the key messages so that employees understand, appreciate and action them to meet our HR and business objectives. But how do we do this? How do we get our employees to take the time and make the effort to absorb and digest our communication messages so that there is a 'shared meaning', which is when they clearly understand what we are saying and what they need to do? In a world where we are all overwhelmed with messages, how do we make ours stand out and be clear enough so that it can be effective and make an impact on our employees and ultimately the business?

Let me answer this question with one word: IMPACT. Through the IMPACT communication model I've created and explained in this book, you will become a more effective communicator, and achieve your communication objectives. Now I can't promise this, giving you a money-back guarantee if not achieved, but that is because this is not a miracle cure. This is a working model, a DIY (do-it-yourself) approach, one which has been developed from my over 30 years as a human resource professional. It will only work if you take some or all of the concepts, lessons and tips, and apply them in a way which will work for your communication campaigns.

So, let's get started. This chapter, like all others in the book, will begin by listing the areas which will be covered, thus setting your expectations. In this chapter we will cover the following:

- Why is communications important?
- What are the objectives of effective communications?
- What are the challenges of communication?
- What is the IMPACT communications model?

Why is communications important?

It doesn't matter what industry you work in, where you are located in the world, or the type of employees who work for you: communications is at the core of everything we do to achieve our HR and business objectives. According to the Chartered Institute of Personnel and Development (CIPD), communications 'supports the organization's smooth running, successful change programmes and good leadership on vision, strategy and values' (CIPD, 2015). For this reason, communications is critical to the success of our organization, and one of the key reasons why it is important to communicate effectively. I've listed in Figure 0.1 some of the other key reasons for creating effective communications:

FIGURE 0.1 Key reasons for communications

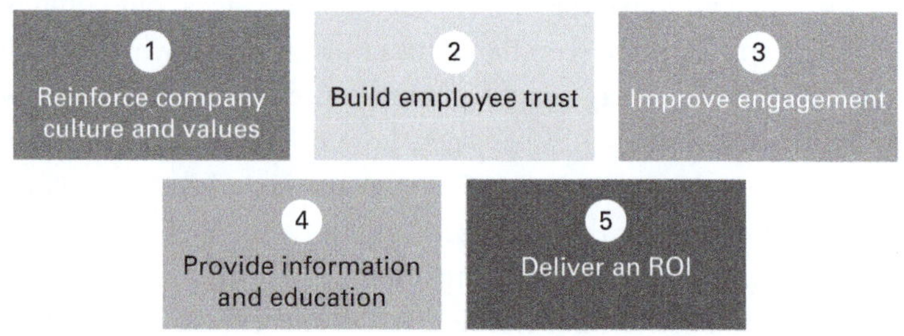

Let's look at each of these key reasons individually.

1. Reinforce company culture and values

Put simply, your company culture and values are the vehicles your organization uses to explain your personality to your employees and to the marketplace. Think of a character in a play, with their personality being expressed in the words they use, the clothes they wear, and the way in which they act. Communicating this personality is key to engaging the audience with the role, and the story which is being told. If this isn't done effectively the audience are confused, fall asleep due to boredom, or simply walk out of the play.

Now think of your employees, and the need for them to understand and relate to your company's 'personality'. Every time you communicate to your employees you are being given the opportunity to do just this, reinforce your personality by aligning your communications with your company culture and values. For this reason your communications with employees is a valuable tool to engage and/or re-engage your employees with this personality and the organization.

2. Build employee trust

Trust has been proven to be an essential ingredient in achieving organizational success. Think about it: if you trust a person, your manager or your company, isn't there a greater likelihood that you will engage with them, and thus cooperate and contribute? Research carried out on Great Place to Work® data by Professor Alex Edmans at the London Business School shows that the 'Best Workplaces' (organizations having higher levels of both trust and engagement than other organizations) consistently outperform the market by between 2 per cent and 3 per cent over a 25-year period (Great Place to Work, 2014).

Helen Wright, Head of Marketing and Communications at Great Place to Work® said to me:

> Communication plays a critical role in building and maintaining trust, with the most important element being the 'employee voice'. Employees need to be given every opportunity to give management their feedback and suggestions, or voice their concerns, knowing they will be listened to and where appropriate acted upon. Communications which are open and honest will also help build trust, as will leaders and management being visible and accessible to employees. This is particularly important in large organizations where the personal approach may be more difficult, but this can be supported through video links, podcasts, etc. Again, this is where building trust in the organization will increase communications' effectiveness.

Further evidence of the impact of communication on employee trust is explained in a paper titled 'The truth about trust: Honesty and integrity at work' by the Institute of Leadership and Management (ILM, 2014). According to this paper the second driver of trust behind openness is effective communication. The ILM research found that 53 per cent of those surveyed believed that effective communication was a powerful driver of gaining and/or improving trust with their employees.

3. Improve engagement

According to the CIPD:

> Employee engagement is a state of being – both physical, mental and emotional – that brings together earlier concepts of work effort, organizational commitment,

> job satisfaction and 'flow' (or optimal experience). Typical phrases used in employee engagement writing include discretionary effort, going the extra mile, feeling valued and passion for work.
>
> CIPD, 2014

In HR we are familiar with this concept, as we read reports and hear talks which discuss and show the positive impact of employee engagement on our organizations. If we go back to the Great Place to Work® report, it cited that the engagement levels in the top 10 ranked organizations were 95 per cent compared with only 42 per cent in the bottom 10 unranked organizations.

So we know that engagement is critical to our organization, but what is the link between employee engagement and communications? How will our communications positively impact engagement? According to Aon Hewitt's 2014 *Trends in Global Employee Engagement* report, communication is one of the five top engagement drivers along with career opportunities, performance, organizational reputation and pay. I'm not surprised by this, for as with trust, engagement is something which can be positively or negatively impacted by how we communicate with our employees. As a key HR objective is to increase employee engagement, communication is a powerful tool to assist us in achieving this important objective.

4. Provide information and education

The first three reasons for communicating to employees are ones from the heart, as they talk about how communications will reach our employees emotionally. This next reason is one of the mind, in that it touches our employees through providing information and education. This is critical, as our busy employees want something of substance, something that will personally help them better understand or action the information which we are providing to them.

For example, if we are rolling out a new bonus scheme, our employees will want to know how it works and what they need to do to impact their chances of receiving a bonus. This information and education is key to them personally, but also to the business. The reason for this is that if employees don't understand how to succeed they will not achieve results, and thus the company will not achieve results. Communication gives us the opportunity to share this critical information with our employees, providing helpful and critical education.

5. *Deliver an ROI*

An ROI (return on investment) is a quantifiable metric which shows the financial return of an investment. From an HR perspective this explains what the business has gained from the time and money spent on our HR programmes. It could be a direct financial measure such as increased profits, or indirect financial measures such as increased engagement or reduced turnover. All of these measures show the business that the HR programmes have delivered results and have contributed to the success of the organization.

What happens if our employees don't understand and/or appreciate these HR programmes, and thus we've missed the opportunity to deliver the ROI? It is through effective communications that we are able to ensure that these critical messages get out to our employees and, as mentioned before, there is a shared meaning. This ROI from communications is seen in a 2014 Gallup survey which showed that 86 per cent of employees who receive clear communications are more motivated to deliver added value. This value, in addition to the benefits cited in the previous points of trust and engagement, add up to deliver valuable ROIs to your business.

What are the objectives of effective communications?

At the beginning of this chapter I introduced the concept of 'shared meaning', which is a key objective of effective communications. The other concept I'd like to introduce is a 'call to action', which can only happen with this shared meaning. This means that your audience knows exactly what they need to do and how they need to feel. It could be a physical call to action, such as going online and registering for a new employee benefit scheme, or it could be an emotional call to action, such as feeling appreciated and empowered by a new employee recognition scheme.

In order to get your employees to the call-to-action step they must move up the communication 'ladder'. I've shown in Figure 0.2 a version of a communication ladder which is used by WorldatWork, a non-profit HR association who focus on compensation, benefits, work–life effectiveness and total rewards. I teach a communications class for WorldatWork, and find this model helpful in explaining how employees must move from one rung of the ladder to the next in order to reach the desired call to action. As you can see in Figure 0.2, you start with awareness (becoming aware of

FIGURE 0.2 The communications ladder

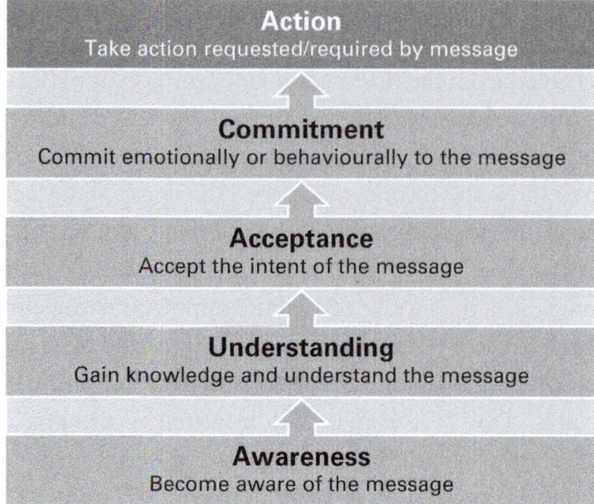

the message) and work your way up through the other rungs of the ladder to reach the final rung, action.

It is our role as HR professionals to create and deliver a robust communication campaign so that our employees can easily move from one rung of the ladder to another. By doing this we will ensure that our messages are understood, accepted, committed to and actioned. Throughout our campaign using the IMPACT model we will discuss how to achieve this ultimate objective.

What are the challenges of communication?

I'd love to say that it is easy to get employees to reach the final rung of the communication ladder, the call to action, but unfortunately it is not always the case. We face a wide variety of challenges throughout our communication campaigns, some of which are within our control and others which are completely outside of our control. Here are a few challenges which I've encountered over the years.

Global workforce

Many organizations operate globally, which means we are being asked to communicate to a global workforce. Even organizations not operating globally may have to deal with a global workforce, as employees may not be native to the country. I'm an example of this, being born and raised in the US, but working in the UK for the last 17 years. Take it from me, even with the English language there are different meanings between these two countries (chips versus crisps, eggplant versus aubergine, eraser versus rubber... the list goes on and on!).

We face a variety of challenges when communicating to global workforces based on differences in language, culture etc. It is important to keep these in mind when developing and delivering your communication campaign, for failure to think through and/or address these challenges can make the difference between succeeding and failing. Here are just a few to keep in mind, that will be covered throughout the book:

- *Think about your words*: With global audiences it is critical to think carefully about the words you use so that they will be understood, and thus actioned. Here's an example of when this was not done so well by a US global retailer. The situation was that the merchandisers were sending written communication to the stores on how to dress the mannequins for the shop windows. They told them to dress the mannequins in 'pants'. Now in the US this means trousers, but in the UK it means undergarments. So what do you think they did in the UK? They dressed the mannequins in undergarments! The good news is that the retailer learned an important lesson, changing their communications to include pictures. But as you can see, selecting the wrong word can have a big impact (mannequins in undergarments!). In Chapter 5 (Content) I will share with you tips on how to select the appropriate words, thus communicating to your global audience effectively.
- *Think about your graphics*: As with words, graphics (eg pictures, colours etc) can have different meanings in different countries, and thus need to be considered when communicating to a global audience. Here's an example of when we almost did it wrong when preparing global total reward statements (personalized statements showing employees the total value of their rewards package). I worked with a team in the UK to draft the cover graphics and colour scheme for the global document. We had selected the colour red as our primary colour in the campaign, for the Western meaning of this colour was energy, excitement and action, which fit our communication objectives. However, when we sent the draft to our colleagues in Japan, we discovered that red had a meaning of anger and danger

to them, which was certainly not the objective of the campaign. We quickly changed the colour scheme, working together as a global HR team to develop a truly global communication campaign.

- *Think about translations*: It may seem obvious that messages need to be translated into different languages, but I've worked in companies before when this was not considered and/or put in the communication budget. If your employees cannot understand the messages, they will not only not be understood, but could actually send a negative message to your employees that the company does not care about them. For this reason, review the need to translate at the beginning, working with your global business partners to understand the translation requirements.

More diverse workforce

In addition to global differences, we also need to acknowledge and address differences based on our diverse workforces. Diversity, whether it is through differences in age, race, sex, national origin, religion etc, means that we need to adapt what and how we communicate to these diverse employee groups. I'm not saying that we need to create different communication campaigns, media and/or content for each individual group. I am suggesting that as we select these we need to take the time to understand both their similarities and differences. Likewise, we need to take a flexible approach so as to develop our campaign to suit the needs and preferences of these groups.

Noise

Communication 'noise' refers to something which influences the ability to effectively communicate. These can be physical or emotional, and can detract from whether or not your communication is heard and thus actioned. A simple way to think of this concept is to remember a game you may have played as a child when you whisper a message in the next person's ear until you get to the end of the chain. Do you remember how funny it was when the message got changed from person to person? This was noise, as it distorted/changed the message as it was sent and received.

An example of physical noise occurred when we communicated changes to two HR programmes at the same time. One was a positive change, and the other a negative change. The negative became the noise, as the positive was not properly heard as employees were focusing too much on the negative message. Had they been communicated at separate times, the positive message would have most likely been received in a positive manner. An example of emotional noise occurred when I worked for a company where some offices were not trusting of the company due to things that had happened in the past. What this meant was that when we communicated a new HR programme which was a positive for employees, it was received negatively. This was due to the negative noise from the employee/employer relationship. As seen in both of these examples, it is important to consider and address noise when developing your communication campaign.

Information overload

Information overload affects us all in our everyday lives. Think about it: how many e-mails, texts, social media messages, phone calls and meetings do you receive or attend every day? It doesn't matter where you live, your age or your job: we are all faced with information coming at us quickly and in many forms. This leads to overload, with too much information for us to manage, and thus messages being ignored and/or discarded. For this reason we need to, as I said at the beginning of this Introduction, find a way to make ours stand out. If it does not stand out it will be put in the 'junk folder' either physically or emotionally by our employees. Throughout this book we will cover ways to achieve this objective through media and content, finding ways so that messages are understood and actioned.

There are a variety of other challenges that we face depending on our company, our employees and/or our individual situations. The key is to take the time to understand them and address them as I will cover throughout the book using the IMPACT model. Together, like a good recipe, they will work together to overcome your challenges and create an effective communication strategy and campaign.

What is the IMPACT communications model?

My experiences developing communication strategies and campaigns, and addressing the challenges I've highlighted have led me to develop the IMPACT communications model. Figure 0.3 presents the model that I will be sharing with you throughout this book.

FIGURE 0.3 The IMPACT communications model

To understand the model and how the book will explain the model, I've listed below some key points:

Helpful acronym

An acronym is an abbreviation formed from the initial letters of other words, and pronounced as a word. Creating an acronym is often a good strategy for helping to remember key information, serving as a memory aid. For this reason I decided to create an acronym for the communications model, creating something which will be straightforward and memorable for us all to use.

The word 'impact' means to have a 'marked effect or influence', so it is the perfect word to use for a communications model. It represents the objective of having communication campaigns that have an effect or influence on our employees and the business. The individual letters stand for the critical phases of the communication process, thus ensuring that we tick all of the boxes that lead us to our success. Each chapter of this book will cover one letter in the acronym, explaining each phase of the communication process.

Non-sequential

It is important to note that the model is not sequential, meaning that the different processes do not happen in a certain order. The reason for this is that from my experience I believe that although there is some order to be followed in communication campaigns, there also needs to be simultaneous actions and/or flexibility in the order. This ensures that you have a joined-up approach to your campaign, which according to Debi O'Donovan, founder of Reward & Employee Benefits Association, is what is demonstrated in best-in-class organizations. I love watching cooking competitions, and always admire how the chefs are able to juggle preparing the multiple courses of a meal, getting it all done at the right times. This is how I like to think of a communication campaign: a complete meal which is prepared and served well, and enjoyed by your audience.

This will make more sense as you read the book, but let me give you a quick example to illustrate this point. Let's say you wait to test the effectiveness of your communications until the end of the campaign, which in the model is Process (Testing). By doing this it may be too late if at the end you find that one or all of your communication messages and media were not effective. By testing at various times throughout your campaign, as I will explain in Chapter 6, you will have a better chance of ensuring you meet your communication objectives.

Expert tips and advice

I have been an HR professional for over 30 years, working for a number of leading global organizations in a variety of industries. Over the years I've led or participated in numerous communication campaigns, and from this I have developed a toolkit of tips and advice on how to manage campaigns effectively. However, I'm the first to admit that I don't know it all, so I have enlisted the help of other HR and communication professionals and consultants to provide even more tips and advice throughout this book. These various dimensions of expertise provide you with a balanced and comprehensive view on how to achieve IMPACT from your communication campaigns.

To assist you further, I've included at the end of each chapter high-level tips to summarize what has been shared throughout the chapter. This will remind you of the key messages to remember and action.

Real-life stories and case studies

One of the best ways to learn is through real-life examples and stories. For this reason throughout the book I've included stories of what I and others have done well and not so well, as these are great ways to illustrate points and concepts. I've also included five case studies from award-winning communication campaigns. These will hopefully inspire you as you create your communication campaigns. I know they inspired me.

'Hats' listed for each job

As each phase in the model involves having to think and act in a specific way, each chapter will provide you with practical insights into how you can do this by wearing the right 'hat' and demonstrating the most useful skills. The 'hat' represents the role/job you will need to perform to achieve the desired results. By wearing these hats yourself, or finding others who can wear them, you will ensure that your project team is equipped to manage your communication campaign effectively and with IMPACT.

To assist you further, at the end of each chapter I've listed the key skills required to perform the role/job. This will help you and the communications project team prepare to acquire the skills needed to action the right 'hat'.

Conclusion

According to Michael Rose (Reward Strategy Consultant at Rewards Consulting Ltd and author of many publications on reward management):

> Communication is critical and often more important than the 'technical' solution. All of my experience tells me that we almost always get the balance wrong between what time and money we spend on designing HR changes and their effective communication. The only solution that will have traction is the one believed in by those leading the change and owned by the organization.

I completely agree with Michael, as communication has a critical and powerful role to play in supporting our HR programmes and our key messages. If done well it can assist in achieving objectives such as reinforcing company values and culture, building employee trust and engagement, providing necessary information and education, and delivering an ROI to the business. The aim of this book is to set you up for success in achieving these objectives. By using the IMPACT model and the tips and tools provided, you can overcome the challenges and barriers you face when communicating your HR programmes, and deliver communications which will have both impact and effect.

References

Aon Hewitt (2014) *Trends in Global Employee Engagement*

CIPD (2015) Employee Communication Factsheet, revised September 2015, http://www.cipd.co.uk/hr-resources/factsheets/employee-communication.aspx [accessed 2 October 2015]

CIPD (2014) Employee Engagement Factsheet, revised December 2014, http://www.cipd.co.uk/hr-resources/factsheets/employee-engagement.aspx [accessed 2 October 2015]

Great Place to Work (2014) http://www.greatplacetowork.co.uk/our-approach/what-are-the-benefits-great-workplaces [accessed 2 October 2015]

Institute of Leadership and Management (2014) The truth about trust: honesty and integrity at work, September, London

Oxford English Dictionary Online, www.oed.com

NVESTIGATION

Investigation

01

Introduction

As Sherlock Holmes once said: 'You should never theorize before you have the facts.' He went on to say that 'you should not twist the facts to suit the theory, but instead twist the theory to suit the facts' (Doyle, 1892). I don't know about you, but in my professional HR career I'm embarrassed to say that at times I've done just what detective Holmes said not to. Because of lack of time, money and/or pressures from the business, I've jumped into launching the communication campaign without taking the time to gather my facts. Sometimes I've been lucky and it has not caused problems, but other times unfortunately I've completed the campaign with some failures thinking 'if only':

- I had discussed and agreed the objectives with key business stakeholders;
- I had thought through how employees would have reacted to the messages;
- I had known about other HR and business initiatives taking place at the same time.

In this chapter I'd like you to wear the hat of a *detective*. The reason for selecting a detective is that they use a wide variety of techniques to conduct their investigation, catch the bad guy and ultimately solve the crime. We in HR can learn from these detectives and use similar investigative techniques to solve our crime and get the right result – or in our case, get the right answers to our questions and ultimately deliver an effective communications campaign.

In this chapter we will cover:

- How to ask questions.
- How to analyse data.
- How to create objectives.

How to ask questions

As any good detective would do, first you need to ask your business partners and employees questions in order to understand them, their needs and the overall situation. Think of any detective book or programme and there is always a scene of a detective interrogating witnesses, suspects etc, pulling out those key nuggets of information by which to solve the crime. Now I'm not suggesting that you use some of the interrogation techniques shown by some of my favourite detectives such as pounding your fists on the table or throwing chairs against the wall (although that could be interesting), but think about how these detectives effectively obtain the critical information and mirror these behaviours instead.

In this section we are going to address the following:

- Why ask questions?
- How to ask the 'right' questions.
- Who are the 'right' people to ask?

Why ask questions?

Mary Astor, a famous US actress, once said: 'Once you ask questions the innocence is gone'. I find this a great way to start out answering the question 'why', as it shows that by asking questions you are no longer innocent, as you have now gained knowledge and understanding. Here are some other key reasons for asking questions.

It defines success

I know it may seem obvious, but you have to have a purpose in order to determine if you have succeeded. As with objectives, which define your communications campaign, you need to make sure that when you finish your campaign it ticks all of the boxes for your audience. You can't gauge your success unless you know why and even how you're doing it.

Here's an example of what I mean from a recent cooking 'incident' at my house. I was very proud of myself, finding a new and exciting recipe for bolognese sauce. I spent an hour preparing it, and left it to cook for six hours in a slow cooker. When I served it to my audience (my husband and son) they were disappointed as they were expecting traditional bolognese sauce. If I had only asked them how they would feel about trying a new recipe, I could have saved myself time and money (as I had to throw most of the sauce away). Another reason for asking for their input is that they may have been more open to the idea of this new recipe, as they would have been a part of deciding to try it.

It assists with decision making

By asking questions you gain valuable information and insight into what your audience is looking for and expecting. This will greatly help you to make decisions before and during your communications campaign.

This is something I experienced when putting in place new benefit programmes at a previous company. We decided to conduct focus groups to not only find out which new benefits our employees would like to see put in place, but how they would like to hear about them. The employees in the focus groups completely surprised me by saying that for each new benefit they would like an e-mail to come from me to launch the scheme. The reason I was surprised was: (a) as I was new to the company I didn't think they knew who I was, and thus thought they would ignore my e-mails; and (b) with all the e-mails they already receive from the business, I thought they wouldn't want yet another one. I was completely wrong, as they said that everyone had heard of me. Rumours were out there that I was putting in place new benefits, so anything received from me would be seen as something positive and exciting. They also said that although they got a lot of e-mails, it was still the best way to communicate to them.

It takes away the 'if only'

As I said at the start of this chapter, the risk of not asking questions is that you get to the end of the project and ask yourself 'if only'. By asking questions you eliminate the use of these two little words.

An example of this is when we were introducing a new HR scheme. It should have been seen as something positive, as employees had been asking for it for quite some time. However, the project team got so focused on rolling it out that we didn't ask the rest of the HR team what they were working on. As it turned out, the compensation team were making a change to weekend pay at the same time, decreasing current rates. This was something that was being made for the right reasons, but employees would definitely see it as a negative. By not asking the HR team the question about timing, what should have been a positive turned into a negative as employees thought that it was only being introduced to offset the negative change. 'If only' we had asked the question about what else was being rolled out to employees.

It engages your audience

One of the key drivers of employee engagement is involvement in decision making. By asking your audience/employees questions, this is exactly what you are doing, making them a part of the solution. Going back to my cooking 'incident', had I involved my husband and/or son in selecting the recipe they most likely would have been satisfied with the meal. My mum used to tell me that I should involve my children in cooking meals for this very reason. They can't complain about the food if they helped make it, right?! Good advice that I should use in the workplace as well.

Another example of this was shared with me by Bill Tompkins, Head of Total Rewards for a $28 billion retail chain. They were communicating a massive change in their US healthcare plan, moving from one kind of a plan to another (traditional PPO plan to high deductible consumer directed plan). They included different segments of employees to help in creating the right messages so that they would resonate with each employee segment (ie executive, part-time logistics etc). This not only acted as a way to engage their employees, but led to them becoming stronger ambassadors for the change and gaining a stronger connection to the communications.

How to ask the 'right' questions

Asking the right questions is key to the success of designing an effective HR communications campaign. A quote by Albert Einstein explains this concept quite well: 'If I had an hour to solve a problem and my life depended on it, I would use the first 55 minutes determining the proper question to ask, for once I know the proper question, I could solve the problem in less than 5 minutes.' By asking insightful questions, or proper ones according to Einstein, you can challenge accepted models, turning the way you think of a situation or concept completely on its head.

A great example of this is the invention of the mobile phone. The story goes that Marty Cooper was tasked by his employer (Motorola) to develop the next generation of car phones. He accepted the challenge, but instead of jumping into the solution, asked himself and others on his team a very insightful question: 'why is it that when we want to make a call we have to call from a physical place?' By asking this question it changed the entire trajectory of his work, refocusing the team on separating the phone from the physical place. The result was that in 1973 Marty made the first mobile phone. It cost $4,000 and had a battery life of just 20 minutes, but it marked the beginning of the era of mobile phones. Now we may not be able to invent something as life-changing as a mobile phone, but we can still learn from what Marty did, and ask these 'right' or insightful questions.

So how do you ask the 'right' questions, keeping in mind that if you ask the wrong questions you will probably get the wrong answers? Here are some tips taken from my experiences, from leading experts as well as from interrogation techniques which detectives use.

Ask open-ended questions

A closed question usually receives a single word or a very short, factual answer. Open-ended questions, however, elicit longer answers. They usually begin with what, why or how, and provide an opportunity for the respondent to give information, opinions, feelings etc.

For example, what response do you get from your children when you ask them how school was? I don't get more than a grunt or a 'fine' if I'm lucky. If, however, I ask an open-ended question such as 'tell me about the activities you did at school' I have a much better chance of getting some real answers and information.

Ask probing questions

Probing questions are used in situations where you need to gain further clarification, or at times when you need another approach for drawing information from your respondents. An effective tool to use when probing is the '5 Whys' method, which was developed by Sakichi Toyoda in the 1930s. The technique helps you get to the root of thoughts, concerns and/or problems.

The 5 Whys is a simple tool to use. You simply ask the question 'why' until you feel comfortable that you have identified the root cause, can identify a solution, or can go no further. You start with the problem, and then ask the question 'why' for each of the responses until you get to a specific answer, and can go no further. You may need to ask the question 'why' five times, or it could be more or less, depending on how long it takes to get to this root cause. In the following example the problem is that the car will not start. Here are the questions which were asked to fully answer the question:

1. Why? The battery is dead.
2. Why? The battery is not changing as the alternator is not functioning.
3. Why? The alternator belt has broken.
4. Why? The belt was very old and had not been serviced.
5. Why? The car was not maintained according to the recommended service standards. STOP HERE: you have now reached the root cause, which was that the car was not maintained.

I'd like to make a point about the 5 Whys, as I think it is important. Whilst I agree that this is a great approach for identifying a root cause and a solution, something to highlight is that you want to balance this technique with respect for your audience. What I mean by this is that sometimes using the word 'why' may put people on the defensive, and could cause them to shut down. I'd suggest keeping this in mind, and should it do so, think of another way of asking the same question. For example, instead of asking 'why don't you like to receive text messages?' say something a bit softer such as 'what is it about text messages that you don't like?' Both of these act as probing questions and get the same result.

Ask leading questions

Leading questions are used when you want to lead people to an answer or your way of thinking, but you also want to make them feel that they are part of making the decision. They are also used when you want and/or need to close a conversation. Do take care when using these, as you don't want your respondents to feel as if they are being either manipulated or forced into a decision.

A way to use leading questions is to give people a choice between two options, both of which you would be happy with. You could say: 'Would you prefer that we send the new HR booklet to your home or drop it on your desk?' In this situation you are still gaining their opinion, but you are not opening it up to a debate on an option such as putting it on the company intranet which you may not be considering.

Other key phrases to use when asking leading questions are 'what if' and/or 'how might I'. These could be helpful in trying to get more details from your respondents, leading them to provide the specifics which you require. For example, let's say you are rolling out a new HR programme and are not sure how much detail to provide (eg a high-level summary or a detailed letter). You could phrase the question as: 'What if we give you a high-level summary of the new HR programme; will this give you what you need?' or 'How might I provide the information to you on the new HR programme?' Both of these questions open the door for a conversation to provide you with information for your communications campaign.

Ask funnel questions

This technique is used when you need to uncover more details on a specific point. It is a common technique used by detectives when questioning witnesses. It has similarities to the 5 Whys, as it asks probing questions; however, it uses a funnel approach by applying different words to get to the solution.

For example, after you ask your leading question about where employees would like to receive the HR booklet, you find that half of them would not prefer the desk drop. This is your preferred option, so you want to understand exactly why they don't want this approach. You've asked the general question (first part of the funnel), but now you need to get more specific information to understand their hesitation and/or opposition. Here are some questions you may ask using the funnel approach:

How many of you have your own desk in the office? Response: Everyone
How many of you are at this desk every day? Response: Only half of respondents
Where are you when you are not at your office desk? Response: Work from home
When you work from home what happens to things left on your desk?
Response: Often it is thrown away.

From this you can now understand why half of them did not want the desk drop, as they were concerned that they would never receive the HR booklet. You can also see the detective-like persistence in questioning which was used.

Focus on a single attribute

According to Dr Andy Brown, CEO of Engage, it is critical when asking questions to focus on a single attribute. This helps in several ways. First, it helps keep respondents focused, rating one aspect of communication at a time. Second, it prevents you 'confounding' two findings. For example, if you ask the question, 'To what extent do you agree that our communications around the new pension scheme were timely and open?' a respondent may believe the communications were done in a timely manner, but not that they were open and honest. So how could they answer the question without giving a false impression on one aspect of the data? Finally, it also makes it more straightforward to analyse your data when you are focusing on a single attribute, as there is no chance of confusing how respondents are rating the two attributes when you separate them out.

Begin with the end in mind

A key to asking the right question is to begin with the end in mind, focusing on what you need to know to achieve your objectives and gain clarity. For example, if an objective is to have high participation in your new employee ideas programme, you may want to ask questions such as:

- How do you like to receive instructions on new initiatives?
- How much detail do you like and/or require?
- Do you prefer written instructions, verbal or face-to-face?

By asking these questions you will be able to understand how to structure your communications so that your employees receive the appropriate instructions and details, and they are given in a medium which works best for them. Had you not done this they may not have had what they needed in order to participate in this new employee ideas programme.

In Table 1.1 I've provided you with some tangible questions which you may find helpful in your organization. I've listed the initial high-level question, and then some further additional questions which you may ask.

TABLE 1.1 The 'right' questions

Initial question	Examples of the 'right' questions
What are the objectives of the communications campaign – why are you doing it?	• Do you want to increase participation in a plan? • Do you want to increase employee engagement? • Do you want employees to understand a change?
What else is going on in the business which will impact the communications campaign?	• Is there too much going on at the time of your campaign so that employees won't pay attention? • Is there something negative which has/will happen in the business which will disengage employees before you have had a chance to engage them?
How does your communications campaign link to the business and/or HR strategy?	• How can you show that what you are communicating aligns with other strategies to represent an overall picture and/or vision? • How can this bring more credibility and/or importance to your campaign?
What has been done in the past at your company which has worked and what has not worked?	• Why was it done this way? • How is your situation similar to the previous situation? • Why did it work or not work?
What has been done externally in the marketplace that you've have heard of which has been successful?	• Why was it done this way? • Is my situation similar? • Will it work at my company?

Please note that this is not an exhaustive list, but is intended to further illustrate how to ask the right questions.

Who are the 'right' people to ask?

Just as important as asking the right questions is asking the right people. Going back to the 'if only' scenario, have you ever completed a communications campaign and thought: 'If only I had asked that employee group or that business leader, I would have done things differently'? This section addresses how to identify the 'right' people, thinking about who will provide you with the most robust thoughts and data. Think like a detective again, asking yourself: 'Who can provide the best clues to help me solve the case?'

Here are a few hints to help you 'select' the right people.

Respondents should represent your audience

Your aim in capturing data is to have it reflect your entire audience, reflecting your organization's demographics. Use your employee data to help you understand your demographic groups, and use this when developing focus groups, interviews, surveys etc. Ask yourself: 'Do I have an adequate representation of all ages, genders, job functions, locations etc?' Make sure you have the right coverage to properly understand any similarities and/or differences between these groups.

Should you be conducting research by an all employee survey, check your responses by demographic groups, ensuring that the results reflect these groups. If not, go back and target specific groups to capture this missing data. It is important to note that if this is not done, your data may be unbalanced and/or biased.

Don't let just anyone participate

It's important to take the time to think about who will add the most value to your investigation. This is not necessarily who will be the easiest to include, either logistically or emotionally, but those that meet your definition of being the 'right' people.

As an example, I was conducting focus groups with employees about the launch of a new HR programme. For reasons of time and money I was being asked to conduct focus groups only in London, as this was where I was based. I pushed back to say that although our London offices were the largest, meeting with employees in some of the more remote and smaller offices would provide a wider range of opinions. By doing this we were able to understand some of the communication challenges and obstacles in smaller offices, and thus structured our communications campaigns in a different and more effective manner.

Consider your leadership team

I've learned from experience the importance of questioning some or all of my leadership team as part of the investigation phase. This is immensely helpful in gaining their perspective and cooperation. Their perspective is helpful for as leaders they often have a valuable and different perspective to you. Their cooperation is also helpful, as they can become ambassadors of change, which was a term I used earlier on in the chapter.

Two other important reasons for involving your leadership team are to get their buy-in and to add credibility to your campaign. Regarding buy-in, if they feel a part of the decisions, you have a better chance of them supporting them and cooperating. Regarding credibility, being able to cite that your leadership team has been questioned in developing your communications campaign will bring a lot of credibility to you and your campaign.

Consider who can/will derail the campaign

According to Dictionary.com, the word derail means to 'cause to fail or become deflected from a purpose' or to 'reduce or delay the chances for success'. Have you ever come across someone who has done this to one of your communication campaigns? I did very early on in my career, and for this reason I always consider these people during the investigation phase of my communications campaign.

An example of this was a campaign where we were rolling out a new HR programme, one where employees needed to actively sign up to participate. A critical part of the campaign was where we had HR team members make a presentation to employees across all our locations, explaining how great this new programme was. Little did I know that one of the team members was not in support of the programme. When we looked at the enrolment statistics we clearly saw the correlation between lack of enrolment and this person's presentations. Had we questioned this person up-front we could have understood why they were not supportive, and adapted how we communicated the benefits to them and to others who thought in a similar way. Alternatively we could have removed them from our presentation team.

Think about your invitations

This final point wraps up the topic of selecting the right people with the step of determining how to handle your invitations. It's important to think up-front about how you are going to invite these important people to provide answers to your questions. The reason it is important is that as you've identified that you need their assistance, you want to ensure their participation or you are back to not having the right information and answers to your questions.

When you send out your invitations, whether it be to a survey, focus group or just an informal chat, you will need to think about how you will explain the reasons for asking for their participation. You need to decide how you will explain the 'whys': why you are doing this and why you are asking the questions. It has been proven that the more open and honest you are, the better chance you have of gaining participation. However, based on your programme/campaign, you need to decide what you can and cannot say up-front, and the pros and cons of an open and honest approach. My suggestion is to start out aiming to be open and honest, and if you find that it will not work, then adjust your approach.

Besides determining what you should and should not say in your invitations, it is also important to determine who the invitations should come from. Should they come from you, from your boss, from a business leader? Ask yourself which name will give the credibility to the communication so that it will be read and actioned. A name can make a big difference, so I would suggest speaking with a variety of stakeholders to gain their perspective on which name will work best.

These hints will help you identify the 'right' people, helping you 'solve the crime' or more importantly for us in HR, achieve a successful communications campaign. They will also allow us to see things through multiple lenses. According to Lesley Alexander, Managing Director of Ferrier Pearce: 'We all come to a situation with our own experience and biases, so it's useful to have other people's perspective in order to get a richer picture.' She reminded me of the existence of the four versions/accounts of a religious story. They all tell us the same story, but do so from different viewpoints and to different audiences. Together they give us a fuller and more comprehensive picture of the events. It's this fuller story that we aim for in talking to the right people, ensuring that we've considered and addressed everything as we develop our communications campaign.

How to analyse data

Fantastic, we've asked the 'right questions' to the 'right people' and now we have the 'right data'. Now what do we do? What you do with this data is absolutely critical to the investigation process, or you end up with data but no answers to your questions. Think of yourself again as a detective solving a crime; picture how they build a storyboard of the crime with their data, helping them eliminate suspects and ultimately find the culprit. Put your data up on a whiteboard (real or hypothetical) and start drawing conclusions. Use the data to draw pictures of what your business leaders are asking for, HR business partners are observing and/or employees are asking for.

Here are some tips on analysing data effectively.

Have an adequate sample size

Before we begin talking about analysing the data, I want to point out the obvious, which is that before we can analyse data we need to have an adequate sample size. Larger sample sizes lead to increased precision and statistically more accurate data. So if you don't have enough data, go back and find a way to obtain more data. The way you do this depends on what method(s) you've used to collect the data. For example, if you haven't had enough respondents to an employee survey, think about a way to coax them to participate. If you don't have enough data from one particular office, consider going there in person and conducting a focus group to obtain this data. Think of what businesses do to get you to complete a survey: they offer you a chance to win a prize. Will this work at your organization?

Here's a joke which addresses the topic of adequate sample size which you may enjoy:

> Three professors (a physicist, a chemist, and a statistician) are called in to see their dean. Just as they arrive the dean is called out of his office, leaving the three professors left in his office. The professors see that there is a fire in the wastebasket.
>
> The physicist says: 'I know what to do! We must cool down the materials until their temperature is lower than the ignition temperature and then the fire will go out.'
>
> The chemist says: 'No, I know what to do. We must cut off the supply of oxygen so that the fire will go out because of a lack of one of the reactants.'
>
> While the physicist and chemist debate which method they should use they are surprised and alarmed to see the statistician running around the room starting other fires. They both scream: 'What are you doing?'
>
> The statistician replies: 'Trying to get an adequate sample size.'

I'd like you to picture the statistician running around starting fires the next time you have collected your data. Ask yourself, would he or she be doing this with my data or do I have enough?

Carefully review your data

Once you have adequate sample sizes of your data, the first thing to do is to carefully review what you have. Read it once, twice, however many times it takes for you to feel familiar with what you have captured. Take notes throughout this step so that you have what you need to progress to the next step. The important point here is to not skip this step, for if you are not comfortable with your data you will end up either making incorrect assumptions or having to revisit your data over and over again. This is not only frustrating but adds valuable time to your campaign.

Organize your data

After you've reviewed the data and feel comfortable with it, the next step is to organize your data. This involves putting the data into manageable groups or sections. The way that statisticians do this is by developing a set of codes. This is helpful as it collapses data to create categories for more efficient analysis, leading you to the next step of looking for how patterns occur.

From a technical perspective, coding data makes it easier for you to sort and analyse the data in spreadsheets. Here's a tip I've learned the hard way: think of how you will code your data up-front so that you only have to code once. Have a discussion with your team, and agree this before you begin the work. It's no fun, and a waste of time, to have to go back and code for a second or third time.

In the example in Table 1.2 I've created codes to be used to review data collected from an employee survey. The questions asked to employees in the survey were about how much they currently know about the pension scheme, and how much they want to know.

TABLE 1.2 Codes for reviewing data

Category	Codes	
Age group	18–25 years old = A 26–35 years old = B 36–45 years old = C	46–55 years old = D Over 56 years old = E
Current knowledge of pensions	No knowledge = 1 A little knowledge = 2	Adequate knowledge = 3 In-depth knowledge = 4
Requested knowledge of pensions	Nothing more = 1 Basic information = 2	In-depth information = 3

TABLE 1.3 Results of data review

Age category	Average Score	
	Current knowledge of pensions	Requested knowledge of pensions
A	1	1
B	2	2
C	2	3
D	3	3
E	4	2

From these codes the data was organized and reviewed as shown in Table 1.3.

Look for common themes, patterns or relationships

Now it's time to step back from the detailed data and look for common themes, patterns and/or relationships that emerge from your data. Statisticians call this 'thematic analysis', and it emphasizes pinpointing, examining and recording patterns or themes within data.

Using the example, once you organize your data you can pull some themes or patterns such as:

- The younger employees (categories A and B) know little about pensions, but aren't interested in learning more. For this group you may want to communicate the basics on pensions so that they become more aware to make the smart short-term decisions about contributions.
- The middle-aged employees (categories C and D) know more about pensions, but as they are getting closer to retirement age they want to know more about this topic. For this group you may want to provide more in-depth communication material.
- The employees nearing retirement (category E) know a lot about pensions and don't feel that they need to know much more about this topic. For this group you may want to give the basics on pensions as a refresher, and then more details on what they need to know as they near retirement and start taking from their pension scheme.

One common way that statisticians conduct thematic analysis is through regression analysis. Regression analysis is a statistical process for estimating and understanding the relationships between variables. Using the previous example, we could use regression analysis to plot the relationship between employee age and knowledge of pensions. We could similarly use this analysis to plot the relationship between employee age and preference in communication medium used. This is helpful when you have a lot of data, and thus you need a statistical tool to assist you with the complex and labour-intensive analysis.

Another thing to keep in mind, according to Dr Andy Brown, CEO of Engage, is not to assume a correlation between data. There may be another confounding factor. For example, if you look at a data set which shows a strong correlation between ice cream sales and homicide rates, you may be making a very false assumption in concluding that the sale of ice cream causes murders. There is, more likely, a third confounding factor, hot weather. We know that a rise in temperatures tends to lead to a rise in the sales of ice cream. Hotter weather conditions are also known to coincide with a rise in homicide rates (*The Examiner*, 2013). In this instance, the relationship between ice cream sales and homicide rates is a simple, statistical coincidence and not a valid correlation.

To pull apart relationships in data properly, there are a couple of ways you can ensure that you are looking at real causation. For example, let's say you are assessing if an increase in senior leadership communications is helping to improve confidence in the future of the business amongst employees. You will need to apply some of these approaches.

Use data which is longitudinal

Use longitudinal data, which is data which has been observed over a period of time, to assess how data and relationships change over the long term. By using this longitudinal data you can observe whether spikes in one particular variable can be seen to have a strong relationship with another over time, regardless of a third confounding factor.

Use smarter analytics

Use statistical modelling tools such as regression analysis to help you assess the impact of one variable on an outcome while controlling for other variables. This is an example of smarter analytics.

Control for potentially confounding factors

Build into your data set any other variables which could be causing 'white noise', meaning there is no correlation in the data, and is just a confounding factor. A confounding factor was explained previously with the example showing that although there was an apparent relationship between an increase in ice cream sales and homicide rates, this was merely a coincidence and was indeed caused by a confounding factor (hot weather). You should try to build in background factors which could be affecting your communications outcomes so as to control for their impact. For instance, if you feel the general performance of a business unit may be affecting how well some of your key messages are landing in those units (eg better performing units are responding more proactively to messages about change), then try to build in an indicator of business performance into your data set. This will help to control for any potentially confounding factors.

Create a meaningful report

After the data has been analysed and themes, patterns and relationships have been established, the next step is to write your final data/observations report. The goal of this report is to convey the complicated data into a meaningful and actionable story. It is important to create this report so that you have a written record to have signed off on, but also to refer to throughout the communications campaign. A suggestion is to make it clear, concise and straightforward. By doing so you will have a better chance for your report to be read and understood. Another suggestion is to have the end in sight, meaning: what do you want the reaction to be to the report? For example, what if you want the report to act as a way for the leadership team to understand the need for and thus sign off on expenses related to a new company intranet site? If this is your objective then you need to make sure that the data strongly and clearly displays this.

This section has focused on how to analyse the data and information you have collected during the investigation phase. By using the tips I've suggested and considering the steps in doing so, you will ensure that the data has been turned from numbers and words into meaningful and useful information by which to create your communications campaign objectives.

How to create objectives

I was taught early on in my career to visualize the end when beginning a project in order to achieve success, looking for the ROI (return on investment) for the business. When pitching projects to business leaders this has been critical, as they don't want to spend the time and money on something that will be of no value to the business. This can be directly financial (eg saving the company money by employees joining a salary sacrifice benefit scheme) or indirectly financial (eg increasing the employee engagement score by engaging employees, thus increasing productivity, through a new recognition programme).

This 'visualization of the end' relates directly to creating objectives, something which is critical to do before you kick off the project. In this section we are going to address the following:

- Why do we need objectives?
- Creating 'good' objectives.
- Gaining agreement on objectives.

Why do we need objectives?

An objective can be defined as something that one's efforts or actions are intended to attain or accomplish. It gives you and your communications campaign a purpose, goal or target. Here are some reasons why it is critical to have these objectives at the beginning of your campaign.

Gives you focus

According to Donald Trump, a famous US business magnate worth $4.1 billion (2015): 'What matters is where you want to go. Focus in the right direction!' This focus is key, for if you use your objectives as the focus or centre of your efforts, you have a better chance of achieving them. Without these objectives you will most likely go in the wrong direction, wasting valuable time and efforts doing so, and ultimately not achieving success.

One way to create this focus for you and your project team is to create a one-page document listing the objectives which you have agreed. Give this to the team to hang by their desk, on their computer, wherever it will best be seen. This creates a visual focus in addition to a mental focus, better setting your campaign up for success.

Resolves issues

Having objectives gives your communications campaign a direction. What happens, however, if in the middle of the campaign an issue occurs which challenges and/or alters your direction? Having objectives can assist with this, as it takes away subjectivity from the situation, focusing you and your team on where you want to get to, helping you find another route.

For example, a company was introducing a new employee recognition programme, and had determined that one of their objectives was to deliver it in a way which supported two-way communication. They decided this as they were concerned that the new programme would be challenging for their employees to understand and thus utilize fully. When the company intranet site they had agreed on was delayed due to programming challenges, they were faced with a decision as to what to do in its place. By revisiting their objective of two-way communication the team was able to resolve the issue and come up with another solution which supported this two-way communication. Had they not agreed this objective they may have selected something which would not have fully resolved the issue, for example selecting a one-way communication approach.

Gains agreement from the beginning

Just as critical as creating objectives is gaining agreement of them from the beginning. We want to make sure that what we deliver through our communications campaign delivers ROI to the business. By having agreed objectives we ensure that we are all heading down the same path together, working towards goals that we all agree are those which should be achieved.

Using the previous example when the communications campaign had challenges which impacted the company's ability to launch the campaign, what would have happened if they had not agreed objectives? They may not have been able to quickly and effectively resolve the issues and the situation.

Enables flexibility

It may seem a bit strange to list flexibility under objectives, as you would expect/hope that once you develop your objectives they do not change. However, you need to be agile and prepared to change direction in a communications campaign, and by having a starting point of agreed objectives, you can better do this.

Using the employee recognition programme example again, what would have happened if the only two-way communication they could deliver in a month to replace the company intranet site was webinars? Yes, this is two-way communications in that it allows questions and answers, but what if the team felt that it wouldn't fully meet their objective of providing comprehensive information? They may need to flex their two-way communication objective to include one-way communication in the shape of an information document to cover the details which would have been included on the company intranet site. By doing this they are flexing their original objective, but doing so in a way that does not compromise the effectiveness of the communications campaign.

Defines success

This was listed as a reason to ask questions, and similarly it is a reason to create objectives. As the saying goes, if you don't have a destination, how do you know if you have arrived? By having objectives you will be able to define and measure your success, celebrating these achievements along the way. I will go into further detail on measuring success in Chapter 6 (Testing), which will explain how to test and measure against your objectives and determine the overall ROI.

Creating 'good' objectives

For a detective it is quite simple to set objectives, as it is to solve a crime quickly and find the criminal. But for us in HR it isn't as straightforward. We need to use the specific data we've uncovered in the data analysis phase, and use this to develop our communications campaign objectives.

One of the most common approaches for setting objectives is the SMART approach. This approach assists us in setting what I've called 'good' objectives, which are ones that will ensure we can deliver an effective communications campaign. As the saying goes: 'If you can visualize it then you can achieve it' – which is what setting 'good' objectives is all about. They help you visualize the end of your journey, so that you know where you are going and are all on the same route.

Many of us in HR are familiar with the SMART approach for setting objectives, as we use it in our performance management systems. It is an approach that has been around for a long time, first mentioned in 1981 in a paper by George Doran. Since then it has been used by others, and in fact the words associated with the letters vary slightly, depending upon who you talk to or what you read. That being said, all parties agree at a high level that well-written objectives help you reach your ultimate goal.

As there are many books on this topic, for the purpose of this section I am going to explain the SMART approach at a very high level. Should you wish to get more details, you can easily find more on this topic in other material/publications.

The SMART approach to setting objectives is summarized in Table 1.4.

TABLE 1.4 The SMART approach to setting objectives

Letter/Word	Explanation
S = Specific	Should be specific rather than general goals, ones which are specific, clear and unambiguous. They should answer some or all of the five 'W' questions: • What – what do I want to accomplish through my communications? • Why – why am I doing this, what is the purpose of my communications? • Who – who needs to be involved? • Where – where is it to be located (eg intranet, social media page)? • Which – which are the requirements and constraints?
M = Measurable	Should contain criteria for measuring progress towards your objectives, and be quantifiable (eg a number, percentage etc).
A = Achievable or Actionable	Should be achievable or attainable, not something which is too far-reaching or difficult to attain. This does not mean that they should not be stretching goals, but ones which can be attained and actioned given the necessary resources and timelines.
R = Relevant	Should be relevant, eg related to other business and/or HR goals. This not only ensures that it fits in with more strategic objectives, but also ensures you will receive necessary support and resources.
T =Time-bound	Should answer the question 'when'. Deadlines are put in place so that the team focuses on the completion of tasks and objectives.

To illustrate SMART objectives, I've listed below some examples from various HR communication campaigns:

- Increase percentage of employees inputting their goals into the performance management system from 75 per cent to 95 per cent of employees. *Note:* This gives the team a specific and measurable objective. My only question would be whether it is achievable to increase from 75 per cent to 95 per cent, but you and your project team would be able to answer this question.

- Develop an intranet site to be available at the start of the performance management cycle (1 December) which contains critical resources and links to the process actions. *Note*: This gives the team a specific timeline as an objective as well as specifics as to what needs to be put onto the intranet.
- Create a multifaceted communications campaign to support the relaunch of the employee recognition programme for 1 January. Campaign should reflect the needs of the key business areas and employee demographics of the company. *Note*: This is a good starting point as it is specific and relevant; however, it needs more details. These could be added once the data has been collected and analysed and multifacets have been determined.

Gaining agreement on objectives

As stated previously, one of the key reasons we create objectives is to align expectations from the beginning. Expectations can only be aligned, however, if we gain agreement on our objectives up-front. By doing this we can ensure that we are not only walking down the same 'path' together, but doing so at the same time and pace.

I can't tell you exactly how to gain this agreement, as it will be done differently at each company. What I can do is provide you with the following guidelines on gaining this critical agreement:

Follow your company's governance structure

Your aim, as with the questioning step, is to ask the 'right' people. Use your company's governance structure to do this, going to those people who are delegated as decision makers. It is also best to ask your campaign sponsor if in this instance there is anyone else that needs to be consulted for agreement. It's always better to involve too many people than too few.

Provide enough details

In the previous section we discussed creating data reports. You and your team will need to decide if these reports provide decision makers with enough detail to make their decisions. You will need to balance providing too little data with too much, with the key being getting this balance right. The last thing you want to happen once objectives have been agreed and the campaign kicked off is to have a decision maker come back and challenge and/or change them.

Give yourself adequate time

Take it from me, it always takes longer than anticipated to get time scheduled with decision makers, and to conduct these meetings. Keep this in mind, giving yourself adequate time to complete these conversations. You may even need to have two meetings with key stakeholders based on how many questions and/or information is requested.

Be prepared for change

Related to the guideline above about time, you need to be prepared for challenges and changes made by decision makers. This sometimes means adjusting an objective, but at times it can mean going back to the drawing board, and reworking one or more objectives. Whilst this may seem like a derailer of the campaign, look at it as an opportunity to get things right from the beginning.

Put it in writing

It is important to document the conversations you have with your decision makers so that you have a record of these conversations. This will not only provide the details for your reference throughout the project, but add clarity should questions arise at a later date. I would suggest that, besides filing these conversation notes in your campaign file, you send a copy to your decision makers. By doing this they will also have a record of the conversation and agreements made.

Conclusion

To end this chapter I'm going to go back to where I started, with Sherlock Holmes' advice to make sure that you collect all of the facts. I've watched enough detective shows and read enough mystery novels to agree with Mr Holmes on this. How many times on these shows or in these books do the characters jump to conclusions and point the finger at the wrong suspect? Just the other day on one of my shows they almost put the wrong person in jail for a crime he didn't commit, only realizing that he was innocent because he had an allergy to the perfume which was worn by the person who was murdered.

Be bold and be brave, and get out there and ask the 'right' questions to the 'right' people. Think of your favourite detective, and their attitude of never giving up, and collect and revisit your data until you believe that it gives you exactly what you want. Use this to create the 'right' objectives for your campaign and for your company, and you will be setting your communications campaign up for success.

Top tips on investigation

- Take the time for investigation, remembering that you can't 'solve the crime' without the facts.
- Cultivate an eye for detail, asking the 'right' questions to the 'right' people.
- Look, listen and smell the 'crime scene', making sure you haven't missed any important clues.
- Be objective and analytical, using data to help you reach your conclusions.
- Revisit the 'crime scene', going back and checking and rechecking your facts and the data.
- Develop robust objectives that are clear, achieveable and deliver an ROI to the business.

Skills for being an effective investigator

- Have an inquisitive personality, thinking and acting like a detective.
- Be open-minded, not jumping or making assumptions.
- Have a forensic approach to data, being able to collect, analyse and make conclusions from data.
- Be resilient and persistent in the face of barriers.

References

5 Whys, https://en.wikipedia.org/wiki/5_Whys [accessed 2 October 2015]

www.dictionary.com [accessed 2 October 2015]

Doran, GT (1981) There's a S.M.A.R.T. way to write management's goals and objectives, *Management Review*, vol. 70, Issue 11, pp. 35–36

Doyle, AC (1892) *The Adventures of Sherlock Holmes*, Harper and Brothers, New York

The Examiner (2013) Climate Change: The connection between hot weather, crime and violence, August, http://www.examiner.com/list/the-connection-between-hot-weather-crime-and-violence [accessed 2 October 2015]

MEDIUM

Medium

02

Introduction

In the first chapter I asked you to think and act like a detective, and in this chapter I'm going to ask you to think and act like a *designer*. From my time working in the retail industry I came to see how critical the designers were to the business. If they designed the wrong article of clothing or selected the wrong colour or fabric, the items would be left on the shelves for the entire season (does anyone remember the season of purple corduroy trousers?). The same is true for us in HR, for as HR communication 'designers' we need to select the medium or media (the plural of medium) that will deliver an effective communication campaign. We don't want to spend the company's time and money developing the wrong 'article of clothing'. We need to get it right, ensuring that, as stated in the Introduction, the message achieves the call to action and the desired outcomes.

With so many media to choose from this makes our lives both easy and difficult. Easy, because we have a lot of choice, and difficult because we have a lot of choice. According to Matthew Hopkins, Communications Consultant, Thomsons Online Benefits: 'The key to selecting the right medium is to do this after the objectives and messages have been determined. You don't want to select the medium first or you may select those which are not appropriate for your audience and/or your messages.' This interrelationship between the medium, objectives and messages are key to the success of your communications campaign. Select the right medium and you will set your campaign up for success from the start.

In this chapter we will cover the following:

- Different types of media.
- Selecting the right medium.
- Getting the right mix.

Different types of media

The word medium can be defined as one or more channels of communication, with the first channel dating back to ancient cave paintings. We've certainly come a long way since the days of cavemen and cave paintings, as today we are spoiled for choice. We have the challenge of trying to keep up with all of the new and exciting media which are being developed and are available.

In this section I will provide information on the various types of media. There are many ways to categorize them, but for the purpose of simplicity I am going to group them into three general categories. Table 2.1 lists these categories and gives examples for each. Please note that this list is not exhaustive, but used to illustrate the categories.

Here are more details on the benefits of each category, and what to consider when using them. You will notice that there is a fair amount of duplication, as the benefits of some are the benefits of others. Please keep these in mind when determining if and when they are appropriate for your organization.

TABLE 2.1 Categories of media

Category	Examples
1 Print	• Booklets • Posters • Billboards • Information sheets
2 Live	• Company meetings • Department/team meetings • Employee orientations • Roadshows • Workshops
3 Digital	• E-mail • Websites • Video • Videoconferences • Mobile devices • Social media

1. Print

Printed channels are any form of printed text and other printed forms such as booklets, posters etc. We use these frequently, and have been using them from the beginning. The benefits of print channels are listed below:

Presents material in a clear and consistent manner

Print material can be very effective at presenting messages in a clear manner, as you have the opportunity to develop content which is concise and direct. This will help your employees easily understand the key messages and turn them into the desirable actions. It is also effective at ensuring that messages are delivered in a consistent manner, as all employees will be presented with the same information.

Provides information on difficult and/or complex concepts

Presenting information on HR programmes can often be challenging, as the concepts can be complex and/or difficult to understand. Print material can be effective in overcoming these challenges as you have the opportunity to clearly present complex information. You can use content and visuals to take the complexity out of the message and/or break it up into meaningful pieces.

Can make documents visually appealing

Presenting visuals can help overcome the challenges of complex information. Print material provides you with the opportunity to present visuals, doing so in creative and innovative ways. An example is trying to explain the concept of a 'salary sacrifice', which is a common way to structure some UK benefits. I've tried numerous times to explain this complex concept clearly, doing so by using various wordings or formats, but the only way I've ever had success in achieving an understanding is through visuals. These visuals are appealing in achieving understanding, but are equally appealing in capturing your employee's attention and interest.

Tangible

A benefit of print is that it is tangible, meaning it can be touched. There is something magical about a tactile experience, being able to hold and touch something. For example, for some the only way to read a book is to purchase it in hard/soft copy, and not to read digitally. Of course, this is a personal preference, but for some people tangible items produce feelings which digital or face-to-face cannot.

Many organizations are getting quite creative with print material and this tactile experience. An example is using a branded sleeve to put around cups. This is a great way to create interest in a communications campaign by bringing the message to your everyday activities (eg drinking your coffee or tea). Another example I saw recently was when a company created a campaign based on the theme of a planet, and created and distributed boarding passes to employees to have them 'board' the new intranet site. Again, a great example of creating a tactile and engaging experience through print.

Can refer to at a later point in time

Print material is often valued by employees as they can refer to it at a later point in time. It can be kept, and filed away in a place where they can easily access it if/when they need to do so. This is helpful as it will allow the messages to continue on, helping employees fully understand and action the messages effectively.

Different

More and more of our lives are moving to digital, so a benefit of print is that it is a bit different. Using print material in addition to other media can bring something to employees which is a bit different, and thus can help make them take notice and thus action accordingly.

Some things to consider when using print channels are:

Time and money

Sometimes as much as we'd like to prepare, print and distribute print material, we just don't have the money. Depending on the size of your employee population and thus the number of documents you need to have distributed, it may just be too costly to use this channel. However, you do have some options to reduce the time and money which are required to prepare these documents. One way is to reduce the size of the documents, doing a shorter version. Another option is not to print the documents, but send them out as e-mails or post on your intranet. I know this changes it from a print channel to a digital channel, but at least you are getting the information out to your employees, and then they can choose whether to print it themselves.

Feedback

One of the challenges with print material is that you are not able to receive feedback from employees from this material. Thus, you do not have a clear understanding as to whether employees understand what is being presented.

However, you do have some ways to receive this important feedback, which is required in your communications campaign. One way is to have managers follow up with employees for feedback, asking them to send it back to the campaign champion. Another way is to have a feedback survey attached to the document, asking employees to complete and return.

Trust

Another challenge with printed material is that it may not elicit a sense of trust from your employees. For some it can be perceived as a bit cold, and thus employees may not feel that you are committed to communicating the true message to them. In addition, as one of the key ways to elicit trust is through listening, and this is not possible through printed material, you will need to find other ways to overcome this challenge. One way you can do this is by using your managers to listen, as was suggested previously for obtaining feedback. This could show your employees that the manager and the company care, and thus build this important sense of trust.

Be green

More and more companies are aiming to run a green business, as it makes sense both financially and from a reputation perspective. This causes questions and challenges about printed material as, depending on a company's green strategy, they may feel that print material does not fit within this strategy. A few ways that you can overcome these challenges are to send out soft copies of the print material (similar to what was suggested in the first bullet of this section) or print on recycled paper and/or print double-sided to halve the number of sheets of paper which you are using.

Perceived value

Right or wrong, some people believe that print is more expensive than other media. For this reason it can create a negative reaction from employees. I experienced this when we presented employees with hard copies of a document during the annual pay review process. I had a few employees who came up to me and said that they would have preferred a pay increase instead of this document. They didn't realize that the document only cost around £20/employee to prepare, as it was their perception that it was a higher cost.

According to Oscar Segovia, Communications Manager – Creative, Thomsons Online Benefits, there are ways to overcome this challenge by not making print material look too glossy and/or expensive.

Efficiency

A challenge of print is that if/when information changes (eg dates, fees, legislation), you need to update, print and redistribute the material. This can cost you time and money, and thus negatively impact your efficiency. A way to overcome this challenge is to make the information more generic, thus future-proofing the information. This will allow it to last longer and require fewer changes. You can provide links to where employees can find the most up-to-date information, for example an intranet site which has this key information.

Here are two examples of when print was used effectively:

Scratch cards

Merlin Entertainments, a leading global entertainments company, used scratch cards to introduce a new employee benefit – a dining and cinema discount card. As Merlin already gave their employees some fantastic benefits through what they call 'Merlin Xtras', they felt that they needed something a bit different and impactful to showcase this new benefit. So in addition to using the normal launch e-mail and posters, they had scratch cards developed to be distributed to all employees. The reason for selecting scratch cards, in addition to being different, was that they wanted their employees to feel like winners by getting this new benefit. As many companies offer the benefit, but ask employees to pay for it, by Merlin paying for the benefit they wanted this positive 'winning' message to come across. This was done very cost effectively and was very well received. In addition, the number of employees contacting the provider for a free card far exceeded expectations, which was down to how well it was communicated to employees.

Total reward statements

Quintiles, the world's largest provider of product development and integrated healthcare solutions, used printed total reward statements in some of their European countries. Although it is common to have total reward statements done online, they felt that it would be more effective as a communication tool to be done in print. The reasons for this were partly due to cost, as they wanted to have them done in multiple countries which would have been quite expensive, especially in some countries where they had small employee populations. The other key reason was due to what was right for their audience. In many of the countries they were not familiar with the concept of total reward statements, so for the first time they needed something which would 'touch' their employees a bit more. This meant being able to have a physical document which managers could go through with employees face to face. This ensured that they not only understood the purpose of a total reward statement, but that the key messages came through and questions could immediately be answered and resolved. Had this been done online this would not have been achieved.

2. *Live*

Live channels are those where a person is talking, and thus can be seen and heard by the audience. They include meetings, presentations, workshops, road shows etc. In this digital age we often move directly to digital when developing our communications campaigns. However, communicating using live channels does something which the other media cannot do, and that is being able to send and receive non-verbal cues. These cues range from facial expressions to body language, and can help you gauge the reaction of your audience to your messages. Other benefits of live channels are:

Provide information on strategic concepts

Communicating strategic information can be difficult, as often you are communicating concepts involving vision, goals, priorities, plans etc. These are not easy to get across due to the complexity, sensitivity and/or emotional impact of these messages. For this reason it is often more effective to present strategic messages in a live setting, providing an opportunity for employees to hear this in person, showing that the business believes the messages to be important to them. Another way to support this is by having a business leader deliver the messages, adding credibility and importance.

A final benefit to point out in respect to strategic concepts is that by using live channels you are able to reach more than one audience at the same time. This is often important with strategic messages as you don't want different groups of employees to receive the message at different times. As you may have encountered, this can cause problems as the message gets changed as it is passed from one person/group to another.

Provide information on difficult and/or complex concepts

Presenting information on HR programmes can often be challenging, with strategic messages, can be complex and/or difficult to understand. Live channels can be effective in overcoming these challenges as you have the opportunity not only to present the information directly to employees, but to handle immediate questions and/or concerns to add clarity when required. You will also be able to focus your audience's attention on the messages, which increases your ability to get your messages across effectively.

Give immediate feedback

Live channels are helpful as you are able to receive, as mentioned earlier, real-time and thus immediate feedback. This can be gained through both verbal and non-verbal cues, as you can hear and see first-hand how employees are receiving and reacting to messages and feel the climate in the room. This is extremely helpful, as you can determine if the messages are being presented in the most effective manner. Another benefit is that it can assist in understanding if/how changes need to be made in future presentations. You can determine if you need to adjust the presentation, material, and/or your tone of voice.

Support conversation and dialogue

Conversation can be defined as 'a form of interactive, spontaneous communication between two or more people'. This is extremely helpful when communicating messages to employees, and can be done effectively through using live channels. This is useful not only to receive feedback, but also to have the interaction and dialogue required so that messages are understood and actions are clear.

Inspire feelings of importance

Think about it: how do you feel if you receive a message in person versus (for example) in writing? Before you even say a word, communicating in person tells your audience that they are important to you, and that the messages, issues etc are likewise important and worth listening to. When you want and/or need to inspire your employees or move them to an action, this is very important, and thus live channels are very effective.

Elicit trust

Linked to the point above about making employees feel important, communicating using live channels can also elicit a sense of trust from your employees. By communicating face to face you demonstrate that you care and respect them, taking the time to personally deliver your messages and respond to their feedback.

Some things to consider when using live channels are:

Time and money

Sometimes, as much as we'd like to visit all of our different locations/offices personally, we may not have the time and/or money to do so. Depending on the number of locations and/or the distance between locations, you may not be able to attend in person. However, you do have some options which may work in your organization. One option is to do what Reward Gateway does, which is to live-stream their meetings to their remote global offices (as shown in the following example). Another option is to film the presentations and distribute them to be shown locally, hosted by a local leader if possible. A final option is to film the presentation and put it on your company intranet, which employees could then view should they wish to do so. These may not be the same as the face-to-face options in that you cannot always receive direct feedback; however, they can still achieve some of the benefits which come from live channels.

Resources

Related to the point above about time and money, if you have multiple locations, you may not have the resources to deliver the sessions. In addition to the number of presenters, you may not have the right people to deliver the sessions. This could be based on their competencies and/or their level in the organization. One way to overcome this challenge may be to conduct training sessions with potential speakers, increasing their knowledge and capabilities. A tip is that in addition to increasing their skills, make sure that they have the buy-in to present the key messages. What I mean by this, and have commented on previously in this book, is that there needs to be a commitment to the messages or the presenter could actually negatively impact them.

Consistency

If you go back to one of the key principles of effective communications content, it is to have consistency. This may be a challenge if you are having multiple people delivering sessions, even if you have one consistent presentation deck. This is due to speakers having different styles and/or levels of understanding. A way to overcome this is to train your speakers, as mentioned in the previous point, but also to prepare additional tools such as detailed speaking notes and detailed FAQs (frequently asked questions). Review these with your speakers and stress the importance of consistency, explaining the implications if presentations are done differently.

Here are three examples of when live channels were used effectively:

In-house global business updates

In this example Reward Gateway, a leading HR technology company who help organizations connect their employees through benefits, recognition and communication technology, introduced a creative way of 'conducting' their global update meetings. Prior to 2012 they had a weekly all-staff meeting in their London office. When they physically could not fit everyone in the room as they grew globally, they moved to a fortnightly in-house TV programme which is presented by two people from a roster of six and recorded every second Friday. It's watched in teams at 9.00 am local time the following Monday in all global offices. An important (and encouraging) note is that they set this all up with no equipment, no training and no prior experience. A team of volunteers made it happen, and according to CEO Glenn Elliott: 'The early episodes were hideously bad; however, everyone loved the intention and the effort.' Two years and 50 episodes later, they now broadcast from their own custom-built studio in the heart of their London headquarters to their global offices. This shows how you can overcome communication challenges as you grow globally, moving from one tradition to another, and creating a modified version of a live meeting.

Global roadshows

In this example a company was making significant changes to their global short- and long-term incentive programmes. These changes could have been viewed positively or negatively, depending on how much employees understood about the current programmes as well as the new ones. It was critical that employees fully understood and appreciated the changes, as they impacted the performance of employees and the company. For this reason the company made the decision to conduct a global roadshow to deliver the information and the messages. Each session was kicked off and chaired by a member of the senior leadership board, who was viewed as a trusted and respected leader. The remainder of the session was led by a senior HR member, as they had the most in-depth knowledge on this complicated topic. This partnership was very effective in gaining the trust and attention of employees, as well as delivering the session in the most professional manner. It also allowed immediate feedback, giving employees the opportunity to ask questions about the changes. A final note is that the sessions involved all levels of incentive-eligible employees, but the group was broken out by job level for the question and answer portion. This was effective in ensuring that employees felt comfortable raising difficult and/or sensitive questions.

Benefit roadshows

A company used roadshows to introduce a variety of new benefit programmes on a benefits portal, as well as to provide information on little known/appreciated existing benefits. As there was a lot of information to share with employees at one time, it was felt that a roadshow would be the most effective way to supplement the new online benefits portal. Benefit providers attended each roadshow, setting up a table with information on each benefit. This provided employees with the opportunity to speak directly with providers, posing detailed and/or personal questions directly to the experts. Each roadshow was hosted by the local HR teams. They handled inviting employees, organizing logistics and adding their own location personality to each roadshow. This meant that they could do something fun and unique which best suited their employee population. In some locations this meant having a barbecue, at another cakes, and at another fun games to play. This was effective in supporting the communications, creating a personal touch to engage employees with the event and the messages.

The outcome was that employees understood and appreciated the full range of benefits offered by the company. This was evident in the increase in enrolment in the benefit programmes, old and new, following the roadshows.

3. Digital

Digital channels are any form of electronic communication such as e-mails, websites, videos, social media and mobile devices. According to CIPD:

> Some of the digital tools on offer today can to some extent create a virtual 'face-to-face' experience such as CEO blogs, following senior leaders on Twitter and webcasts to name but a few. The advantage for many organizations is the degree to which this presents senior leadership as human and 'in touch' – and there is some evidence to suggest that the feeling of a personal relationship with the CEO impacts engagement positively.
>
> CIPD, 2010

In addition to the reasons given in the CIPD report, another key reason why digital is so important as a communications medium is due to prevalence. Let's face it, everywhere you look from a personal or work perspective, you encounter digital communication. According to Ofcom's 2014 *UK Adults' Media and Attitudes* report, over 8 in 10 of UK adults (even older adults) are going online on a variety of devices. According to the 2014 Deloitte *Mobile Consumer Survey*, one in six UK adults who own a smartphone (equivalent to about 6 million people) now looks at their device over 50 times a day. It also shows that the smartphone application that is used first thing in the morning by most respondents is SMS (accessed first by 33 per cent) followed by e-mail (by 25 per cent) and social networks (by 14 per cent). There are many other examples of reports showing similar statistics, all showing that digital communication is on the rise, and thus needs to be considered.

The benefits of digital channels are:

Present material in a clear and consistent manner

As with print, most digital material can be very effective at presenting messages in a clear manner, as you have the opportunity to develop content which is concise and direct. This will help your employees easily understand the key messages and turn them into the desirable actions. It is also effective at ensuring that messages are delivered in a consistent manner, as all employees will be presented with the same information.

Provide information on difficult and/or complex concepts

For some digital channels (eg e-mails, websites) you can overcome the challenges of presenting information on concepts which can be complex and/or difficult to understand. This is because, as with print material, you have the opportunity to clearly present complex information in a clear format. You can use content and visuals to take the complexity out of the message and/or break it up into meaningful pieces.

Can make documents visually appealing

Presenting visuals can help overcome the challenges of complex information. For some digital channels (e-mails, websites) you can present visuals in creative and innovative ways. Keep in mind, however, that due to digital formatting visuals may be challenging (eg viewing an e-mail on different devices), so use them if/when they are effective. As my husband, who is an app developer, always reminds me, test your communications on all devices or you may regret it later as it may not work.

Can refer to at a later point in time

Digital material, like print material, is often valued by employees as they can refer to it at a later point in time. It can be filed away electronically and/or printed out and filed so that employees can easily access it if/when they need to do so. This is helpful as it will allow the messages to continue on, helping employees fully understand and action the messages effectively.

Give immediate feedback

For some digital channels you are able to receive immediate feedback, which is helpful in understanding quickly if/how messages are getting across to employees. This can be one-way (eg you ask employees specific questions on your intranet) or interactive (eg you have a two-way conversation with your employees through social media). Both help you decide if/how messages and/or medium need to change, and allow you to make the changes immediately to meet your communication objectives.

Offer efficiency

Digital channels can be easy to update quickly, meaning you will be better able to react and respond to changes which are required. With print channels you can have a time-consuming process, whereas with digital channels the changes can be immediate (eg with intranets) or more quickly (eg e-mail, SMS). This can save you time and money, and also ensure your employees have what they need in a timely manner.

Enable evaluation

Some digital channels can provide you with data to assist in evaluating usage (eg hits to a website), and thus a means of measuring their effectiveness. This is helpful for a few reasons. The first is related to the previous point regarding efficiency, for if we can understand usage we can evaluate if the communication has been designed effectively. If it is not, we can then make changes. The second is to act as a way to provide the business with data to illustrate the value of our HR programmes. As showing this value is requested and/or expected more often, digital channels help us do this quicker and more effectively.

Create an experience

Some digital channels can create an interesting and exciting user experience for your employees. As Vicky Edwards, Communications Manager – Consulting, from Thomsons Online Benefits pointed out to me, with digital you have so many more options for creating a 'wow factor' which makes your communications stand out and get noticed. One way Vicky suggested doing this is by using interactive content which responds to what an employee is interested in, creating 'active' engagement. Another way is by presenting visually striking communications in a way which is new to employees, generating immediate interest.

In addition to the 'wow factor', when using digital channels such as e-mails and websites you can add more functionality to the user experience. Examples are links to videos, personal information and additional websites. This puts the experience in the hands of the user, letting them decide what is important to them (as mentioned above by Vicky when listing interactive content). Just as important, these links can create effective calls to action, which is explained in the next point.

Achieve call to action

Many digital channels are effective at achieving a call to action which, as we know, is a key objective of our communications. They do so in a variety of ways. One way is to make it so the call to action needs to take place before the employee can leave the channel. For example, you can build in rules so that an employee cannot leave the website until they have completed the desired action. I've used this technique with online performance management and benefit enrolment systems, and it has been extremely effective in achieving the call to action. Another way is to highlight and/or make the call to action stand out in the message. For example, when sending out an e-mail, put it in the subject header (eg 'Open enrolment begins – register by end of October'). Yet another way is to make use of an SMS (short message service). SMS messages are extremely useful in delivering alerts and reminders to your employees, giving them a nudge/push to take an action. As mobile phone users have access to their devices constantly, you have a good chance of having the messages received and read instantly.

Some things to consider when using digital channels are:

Time and money

As with print material, some digital communications can be costly to prepare, which will prevent you from using this channel. However, you do have some options to reduce the time and money required to develop these channels. The first question to ask yourself is, can I switch from one channel to another? For example, if you can't film a video could you create an e-mail? Another option is to create a 'light' version, meaning it doesn't have all of the costly elements. For example, if you don't have the time and money to build a full website, think about if you can build something very basic instead. Challenge yourself to think of the 'light' version.

Availability

Although, as stated at the beginning of this section, a high percentage of people have access to digital technology, you still need to think of availability. For example, if you are sending out an e-mail to work e-mail addresses, will all employees have access to a work computer to receive the e-mail? At a recent conference I heard a mobile company explain that many of their employees spend the entire day in their service vehicles, and thus don't have access to computers/e-mails. If this is the case you don't necessarily need to rule out this medium, but you do need to think of an alternative way of communicating to these employees. Also, remember my example about sending out a video as a way to communicate, and finding out that the computers playing the videos didn't have sound? Yes, employees had availability to receive the video on their computers, but not full availability as they could only see the video. You can overcome this challenge by using additional media. Another way is to set up kiosks for employees to use if they don't have work computers (eg in a distribution centre or a retail shop), thus giving them online access.

Knowledge

In addition to checking availability of digital technology with your employee population, it is also important to check their technology knowledge. What level of knowledge (and even acceptance) do they have with the technology? For example, based on your demographics, would your employees feel uncomfortable accessing important and confidential information via a website? Could you spend time and money creating amazing technology and then find that it is not utilized? I see this as a challenge and not an obstacle. One way to overcome this is to build into your communications campaign ways to educate your employees to feel more comfortable with the technology (eg instructions with screenshots, webinars). You could also build in support networks to assist them once the technology is up and running (eg helplines, local champions). This may take more time and effort in the short term but it could help you for this campaign and others in the future.

Resources

A benefit of digital channels is that you can update them quickly, keeping them up to date and fresh. Whilst this is great, it does require resources to handle the work. If it is not done in a timely manner, this benefit can turn into a negative as the information is incorrect. Another challenge is that digital channel development and maintenance require a knowledge of technology that your team may or may not have. For this reason you need to consider whether or not you have the right resources. You can overcome this in a few ways. The first is to consider maintenance when developing material, making it as easy as possible to make updates. Another way is to train your team on the technology and/or bring in experts to supplement your team so that you have the right skills.

Compatibility

Have you ever been frustrated when using digital channels due to compatibility issues? This could be because the software programs cannot work together on the same system, network etc and/or because one can prevent the operation of another. When this happens the communication media and messages can quickly lose their impact and credibility. An example of this was when a microsite was developed at a company to contain information on their benefit programmes. Through testing they found that, although it worked perfectly on the testing laptops, different locations had different versions of the browser on their computers, which meant the microsite could not be viewed. They resolved this by installing new browsers, and thus overcame the challenge. The point to make here is that you should check the technical requirements of your technology before rolling it out.

Design considerations

The previous point regarding compatibility talks about challenges with different operating systems/browsers. Design considerations talks about challenges between devices (eg mobiles versus tablets versus laptops). Each device has a different shape from the other, and thus the content may fit on one but not on the other. For example, a document that may be clear and readable on a desktop computer might not be legible on a tablet, and content readable on a tablet might not resize properly for a mobile. The point is that you need to take these into consideration, and work with your technical team to make sure that your content fits all devices, or restrict the content to particular classes of device.

Here are two examples of when digital channels were used effectively:

Visual storytelling

In this example Thomsons Online Benefits, who have revolutionized the benefits market through their Darwin platform, helped one of their clients develop digital pensions communications. The company's problem was that they had low understanding and appreciation of the pension scheme, with a very broad range of employees. To engage and educate employees they utilized 'visual storytelling' in the form of a 'parallax' scrolling website as the centrepiece of a digital-led campaign. The scrolling website was designed to follow the typical journey of an employee, taking into account pension-related considerations during different life events, such as a change in tax band, or buying a property. A scrolling website places control of 'when to move on' and which areas to focus on in the hands of the employee. Within this website, links to additional information/resources put further control of information in the hands of employees. This meant they could decide what was of interest to them and their personal situation, creating a more meaningful and emotional connection with the material. This was a break from the typically heavy pension documentation which employees had not engaged with in the past.

Social media platform

This example shows how Reward Gateway has evolved its employee engagement platform to include a social media element. By adding social media to the home page, their clients can offer employees the opportunity to comment and share stories on how they've used the voluntary benefit products. As with other social media platforms, others can 'like' these comments/stories, thus adding credibility to the use of this benefit. In discussing this with Lisa Turnbull (Communications Manager, Reward Gateway), she states that the power of social media on their platform is that it 'makes the programme more human, using the power of word of mouth as a way to engage employees'. She further states the benefit of having conversations made in real time/instant, so that employees can quickly and easily action the suggestions made by others. With a benefit scheme such as voluntary benefits, this is critical as you want your employees to know how and when to obtain these discounts on products. This is an example of how social media can be effective at having your employees market and communicate HR programmes to fellow employees.

4. E-mail

E-mail is still the most common digital medium used by most organizations. According to WorldatWork's 2015 *Trends in Employee Recognition* survey, e-mail was the most common way to communicate recognition programmes (70 per cent), which is an example of its popularity. This is probably because it is the most familiar and often the easiest method.

Some things to consider when using e-mails are:

Make them short and to the point

Chapter 5 (Content) highlights the importance of making messages short and to the point. This is even more important with e-mails for a few reasons. First of all, think of the number of e-mails you receive each day. Your message to employees needs to compete with these, so you don't want to turn employees off with a long and complicated e-mail. Some employees actually decide which e-mails to read (and delete) based on the preview alone, so keep this in mind when you create your subject header and first paragraph. Think of yourself as a gardener, trimming your plants so that they look good and grow properly, and 'trim' your words to make them more effective.

Another reason is due to technology: sometimes e-mails are read on a computer, but often they are read on smaller devices such as mobiles or tablets. With these devices it is more difficult and frustrating to read longer e-mails, having to scroll down to get to the bottom. It can also be difficult to read images and/or banners. Keep these devices in mind when designing your e-mails.

Focus your message

Related to the point above about keeping things short and to the point, you need to focus your message. Read through the tips listed in Chapter 5 on Content, and create messages for your e-mail which clearly create a call to action, focusing your audience on exactly what they need to know and action. A few ways already mentioned include creating impactful subject headers, using fonts, colours etc to create interest and action, and using links and/or attachments as a way to replace unnecessary immediate text.

Anne Allen, People Experience Director at Xero, the accounting software company, tells us: 'The biggest mistake you can make is to assume it has happened.' Repeatly your message is essential, and is a great way to focus your message on the 'call to action', letting your employees know that it is important. For example, if you have an important deadline, you can put it in the subject header and then again at the end of the e-mail, or after the first paragraph so it is visible in the e-mail preview pane (possibly in a different and/or bold font).

Target your messages to your audience(s)

In discussing e-mails with Esther Crew (Director, Performance and Engagement Limited), she pointed out the need to target or segment your e-mails to your audience(s). In Chapter 5 I talk about the guiding principle of relevance. You need to ensure that the e-mail is relevant to the employee, not just taking the easy way and sending it out to everyone. A good tip which Esther shared with me is to follow the 'need to know' rule. Ask yourself: Who needs to know? Before pressing send, ask yourself the following questions:

- Will the business suffer if this e-mail isn't sent today or at all?
- Will my message motivate my employees and/or have a positive impact?
- Would my team, line manager, CEO etc appreciate receiving this message when they are reading it tonight after a long day?
- Does it add value?

If you can't answer yes to one or more of these questions you should reconsider whether the message is important at all. If you can answer yes for some employees but not others, then consider segmenting your e-mails, sending different ones to different audiences.

Consider spam

Spam can be defined as irrelevant or unsolicited messages which are typically sent to a large number of people for the purposes of advertising, spreading of viruses etc. Because of the large volume of e-mails sent these days, often e-mails which don't even meet this definition go into your spam folder automatically. For this reason it is important to consider this, speaking with your in-house technology people to understand how to prevent this from happening. You don't want your lovely e-mail to go into someone's ignored spam folder, right?

5. Intranet/Portal

The intranet is an information system, website or web application with the same flexibility and power as the internet, but is dedicated to your internal employees. It has a restricted group of users, your employees, and thus only they can have access to the content which you make available. Intranets have quickly become a common way to communicate to employees. According to the WorldatWork's 2015 *Trends in Employee Recognition* survey, the intranet is used by 66 per cent of companies to communicate their recognition schemes. This is only slightly below e-mail, which was reported by 70 per cent of companies. A portal is used to further enhance functionality, as you can use it to provide links to different sites or pages on the intranet containing useful information and tools. One of the main differences between an intranet and a portal is that a portal consolidates many intranets. For the purpose of this section I am going to talk about both of these, as the suggestions apply to both.

Some things to consider when using an intranet/portal (called 'intranet' going forward) are:

Keep them simple

I've said previously that words and graphics need to be kept simple, and the same is true for the technology behind your intranet. It is important to select and develop a simple and straightforward platform so that it is a user-friendly medium/tool for your employees. I've seen some that are so complex that they prevent a positive user experience. Remember, if you want your intranet to be effective your employees need to be able to use it and find what they need. Think about your audience, and build it around their needs.

When describing this let me tell you about my husband's new electric car. For him it is an amazing machine, with lots of buttons and tools to help him drive in a smart and cost- and environmentally-effective manner. For me it is a lovely looking car that I will travel in, but not drive, as all the buttons/tools intimidate me. You don't want your 'car' to sit in the driveway; design your intranet to be simple and accessible.

Keep it fresh

Picture an amazing intranet, with lovely branding, graphics, interesting text and helpful links. Now picture clicking on a link that has, for example, old rates for benefits and last year's enrolment deadlines. From my perspective, and I'm sure from your employee's perspective, this is not acceptable! If you are going to have an intranet, then you need to take responsibility for taking care of it, and keeping it fresh with current information.

Training is key

Just as important as designing your technology to suit your employees is designing your training to meet the needs/knowledge of your employees. Think of the previous example of my husband's new electric car. If I was trained in how to use the car I would feel more comfortable driving it. Without this, again, I'll just look at it or sit in the passenger seat, and thus not get the full user experience. So find the best way to train your employees, whether that is face to face, user guides etc and invest in training on your technology.

Pay attention to security

One of the benefits of an intranet is that you can share sensitive and/or confidential information with your employees. With this, however, comes the responsibility of protecting this, and thus putting in place appropriate security measures is key. Work with your IT department to put these in place, and set up ways to monitor and maintain them going forward.

6. Mobile phones/SMS

SMS (text messaging) is a fairly new type of communication medium for HR professionals, but has been used for quite some time by marketers and other industries. As texts have become a common and accepted way to communicate across all age groups, it can be an effective and simple way to communicate messages to your employees.

Some things to consider when using mobile phones/SMS are:

Choose your words wisely

When using SMS we have no choice but to make them short and to the point as there is a 160-character limit. But we do have a choice on what to say within our word limit. It is important to choose your words wisely, making sure that each and every word is adding value, and is supporting the objectives of the message. Think of yourself on a word 'diet': you want to use your word 'calories' wisely, not wasting them on something which is not going to bring you enjoyment or purpose. Also, remember that SMSs are normally used as a 'call to action', so ensure that this is clear in the words you select.

Consider timing

The timing of your message can/will have an impact on whether or not your employees will open and read it. This is certainly true with other media such as e-mails, but it is even more important with SMS thanks to the alerts that go along with them and the fact that most people have their mobile phone with them at all times. It is important to think about work patterns in your office, and understand and respect them when sending out your messages. Also, consider the impact of sending messages outside of work hours, and decide if this will be accepted by your employees or will agitate/anger them. The point here is to consider the timing, and act based on what will work best at your organization.

Consider frequency

Think back to my earlier definition of the word spam when talking about e-mails, explaining them as unwanted messages that are ignored when they go into the wrong folder. You want to make sure that your SMS messages are not considered spam to your employees, and thus ignored. Be selective about when you are using SMS or they will lose their impact. For example, if you are sending an SMS to remind employees to attend a benefits fair, do you need to send two or will one get the point across? Consider your employees and consider and address the frequency.

7. Social media

Social media can be defined as websites and applications that enable users to create and share content or to participate in social networking. According to Ofcom's 2014 *UK Adults' Media Use and Attitudes* report, two-thirds (66 per cent) of online adults say that they have a current social networking site. Nearly all have a profile with Facebook (96 per cent), with an increase in those having additional profiles through Twitter, YouTube, WhatsApp etc. It remains a popular pastime, with 60 per cent of users visiting sites more than once a day, increasing to 83 per cent for those aged 16–24.

I could go on and on with statistics to show the increase in the use of social media, but you probably personally and/or professionally know this already. So how do we feel about social media's role in HR communications? Do we feel that social media has helped or disrupted how we communicate with our employees? The answer is both, as it has greatly changed how and when we communicate to our employees, giving us a tool which we need to understand how to use effectively as it is so different. As said by Susannah Clements, Deputy CEO CIPD, in the 2013 CIPD report, *Social Technology*: 'Responsiveness and agility are two very key issues in our world today – and social media tools can help organizations become more innovative and responsive to change.' She goes on to say: 'Social media activity is about being part of something larger than ourselves. It is less narcissistic and more collaborative than it is given credit for.'

Some things to consider when using social media are:

Consider consequences

One of the reasons why social media has gained popularity is that it allows employees the opportunity and vehicle for two-way communication with their employer. This is helpful for organizations and valued by employees as it gives them a voice. Whilst two-way communication is valuable, it can also cause challenges and/or problems if not done at the right time or in the right way. For example, if you are communicating the closure of an office you need to consider the consequences of using a visible two-way communications vehicle such as social media. Could negative comments posted on social media 'fuel the fire', meaning other employees become upset by reading these comments? Now I'm not saying that these same emotions would not occur by employees talking to one another; they very well could. What I'm suggesting is that before deciding to use social media you should think of whether or not it is appropriate, and if so, how you will manage reactions, good or bad. A benefit of social media is that you will have a chance to respond, unlike employees talking amongst themselves, so think through how you will manage these conversations.

Think of the pace

Social media is fast-paced, which is good, but this also brings challenges. You need to be prepared for, and have resources to keep up with, the pace, reacting to and managing these two-way conversations. As in the previous point, be prepared to react quickly to comments, positive and negative, thinking through in advance how you will address as many scenarios as possible. A suggestion made to me by Matthew Hopkins, Communications Consultant at Thomsons Online Benefits, is to create and train users on general guidelines (not being fully prescriptive) on what can/should be said and what should not – setting you up to effectively manage comments. This will leave users free to respond confidently, quickly and naturally to comments. This is preferable to considering responses on a case-by-case basis, which wastes time and resources, while often negating the effectiveness of the response. This means that effective social media planning not only helps in managing the pace, but also brings you and the campaign credibility, as employees will see that you are reacting in a timely manner.

Another thing to consider when managing the pace is resources. You need to consider who is going to manage the various social media channels, ensuring this dedicated resource(s) is trained and prepared to manage effectively. According to Oscar Segovia, Communications Manager – Creative from Thomsons Online Benefits: 'Not managing social media well is like hanging up the phone on customers with lots of people watching'.

Have a policy

As we know in HR, policies are required and are helpful in many situations. Such is the case when it comes to social media, for due to the highly visible nature of this medium, it is necessary. A key reason for this is that, as social media is used in both work and personal situations, employees can mix business with personal use of social networking in error. By developing and sharing a social media policy with employees you are protecting the company's reputation, as well as ensuring that there is no confusion as to what can and cannot be posted on social network sites.

Selecting the right medium

According to Walt Disney, the famous US cartoonist: 'You can design, create and build the most wonderful place in the world. But it takes people to make the dream a reality' (The Disney Institute Blog, 2014). This quote reminds me of situations when the wrong communication medium was selected and designed, and thus the objectives of the communication campaign were not met. Using Mr Disney's concept, the employees didn't come to what we had built, so our objectives did not become a reality. According to a CIPD paper: 'What we need to keep in mind is that communication is about creating meaning. This is important because the digital revolution has given us many more channels and it is easy to be caught up in the fascination of what is possible and not consider whether the channel is fit for purpose' (CIPD, 2013). This is so true, for the concept of 'fit for purpose' is key in ensuring we meet our communication and business objectives.

In this section I am going to provide you with tips on how to determine what is or are the best media for your organization and your communications campaign. To do this you'll need to think and act like a designer again. It doesn't matter if you are a fashion designer, a graphics designer, an interior designer, or even someone like Walt Disney, who not only created fantastic cartoons but designed the concept of Disney World. You do this by selecting the medium/media which will 'fit' your specific audience(s).

Fit your project objectives

During the investigation phase of your project you will have gathered data and information to understand the needs of your business and your audience(s), as well as develop your project objectives. When selecting your medium it is critical to refer to these objectives, constantly checking in to make sure that you are using a medium which will ultimately enable you to effectively meet your objectives.

An example of this was the objective that BT had for their communications campaign of ensuring that employees got the right information at the right time to make the right decisions at the maturity of their 'saveshare' plan (see case study on p 171). With huge potential profit within their employees' reach and complex decisions to make, BT ran a year-long communications programme using a variety of media to give their employees the tools and information needed to make informed choices on maturity. Examples of media selected were e-mail, webinars, e-chats, newsdesk articles, portal etc, all working together to achieve their project objectives.

Another way of thinking about it is: What is the 'ambition' of your communication? What effect are you looking for after you have communicated? Do you want increased knowledge, better understanding, more motivation or involvement, or do you want to lead them to an action? Use the answers to these questions to help you select the medium which will help you achieve these objectives.

Fit your company culture

When I talk about culture I'm referring to how you define your culture to your employees, whether it is through values, mission statement, whatever it is that you share with your employees to explain who you are and how to act as an employee. When selecting the appropriate medium for your company it is important to think about how they will sit or fit against your culture. For example, does your culture talk of and value transparency and honesty? If yes, then social media, for example, may work well as an effective medium. If your company is more rigid and structured both in the business and culture, you need to decide if social media would be appropriate.

An example of this is how Reward Gateway selected media for their communications campaign involving the selection of a new investor (see case study on p 199). Having a strong culture of open and honest communication, they selected media which supported this, acting in a transparent manner. For example, they created videos throughout the selection process telling the story of what was occurring, keeping their employees fully informed along the way. This worked well for them to support their communication objectives, but may not have been the right thing to do at a company with a different culture.

Fit your audience

As Debi O'Donovan (Founder of Reward & Employee Benefits Association) said to me: 'You need to know your audience to know what will make them sit up and take notice'. Depending on your audience, some media will make them take notice and others will be less effective. Sometimes decisions are based on practical needs, eg employees are on a shop floor and thus don't have access during the day to technology. Other times decisions are based on preferences, eg you have a young workforce who said in your employee survey that they want to be communicated to through an intranet and social media. Together these factors help you decide what will create the impact and effect you require through your communication media.

I saw this point illustrated well at a recent HR conference I attended. I sat through four different sessions on communications, with each company selecting very different media based on their very different audiences. For example, one company was a law firm, where the HR presenter explained that their audience expected very traditional media to be used (eg letters, e-mails and posters). Another company was a technology business, where the presenter explained that the audience expected digital media to be used (eg intranet, social media etc). The key here is to consider your audience and select what will best fit their needs.

Fit your timeline

The final consideration for selecting the right medium concerns your timeline. What I mean by this is that it is important to understand what you can and cannot do based on your communications campaign timeline.

For example, if your objective is to quickly get a message out to your employees about a critical and timely change in their pension scheme based on a legal change, you probably won't have time to create media such as videos, web pages etc. In this example you may want to use written communications to ensure all employees quickly receive the critical information and possibly, depending on your company, a meeting or webinar to add the more personal touch as well as a two-way communication. If the pension change is something which needs to be an ongoing message, then take the time once you've done this to create more lasting communications through web pages etc. Another example may be that you want to build a portal for your new HR programme. However, if you don't have time to do it properly then it is best not to include it in your campaign, as a badly constructed portal could have a negative impact on the programme. If you still feel strongly that the portal is required in order to meet your objectives, then adjust your timeline to ensure you can do it well.

Getting the right mix

Now that you've selected the right medium or media for your communications campaign, the next step is to create the right mix of them. Think of yourself as a baker, mixing together the right ingredients to create, let's say, the perfect bread. If you get it wrong your recipe is an absolute failure, with your bread not rising, tasting too doughy etc. Now think of your media as the ingredients for your recipe, or for us as HR professionals, our communications campaign.

So how do you do this, how do you create the right mix? When it comes to communications, unfortunately there is not one recipe to create the most effective communications campaign. However, you can create the recipe and mix which is perfect for your organization and your employees by doing the following:

Consider purposes

Map out the purpose of each medium, asking yourself what it is that you are trying to achieve, and make sure that they all have different purposes. Figure 2.1 gives an example. What this does is ensure that each medium has a unique purpose, and gets the attention from your employees that you require. If they all do the same thing, for example like baking soda and baking powder in the bread, you are not using them effectively.

FIGURE 2.1 Purpose of each medium

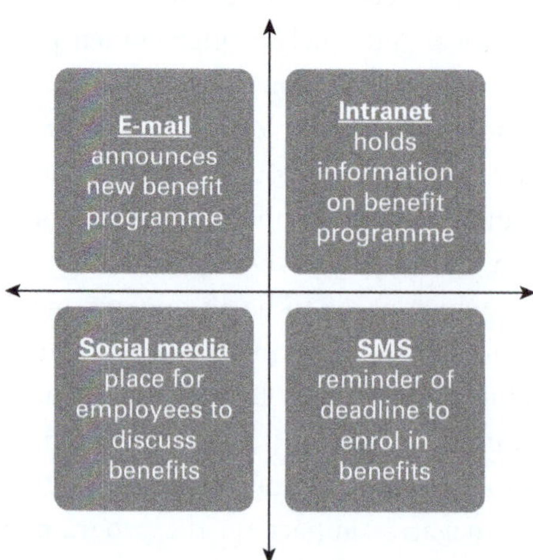

Review your audiences

Another key consideration for getting the right mix of media is to review your audiences once again. What I mean by this is that you need to consider if each medium is going to be effective with each of your audiences. If it is not, then you may need to ignore what I've just said, and use multiple media to convey the same message. For example, if half of your population have access to e-mail and half don't, you may need to use two media to remind them of a deadline. You need to balance this with the previous point about the purpose of each medium, and make sure that you have the ingredients and mix that will deliver the best bakery product, or for us in HR, the most effective communications campaign.

Consider time and cost

When selecting your mix you need to make practical decisions as to whether you have the time and cost for each 'ingredient' or media. As you will most likely have a project budget, you need to review the overall time and cost required of your selected media, and decide if they fit within this budget. If they don't, then you need to decide which will deliver the highest ROI to the overall project objectives, and select accordingly. This can often be difficult and challenging, but using ROI will help you focus on selecting what is most appropriate and effective.

Consider compatibility

A final suggestion is to consider how the various media work together, not being in competition or in conflict with each other. As with any recipe, you want your ingredients to work well together, and not make another ingredient go wrong. Using the bread example, if you put in too much yeast you could cause your bread to rise too much and then collapse, which is certainly not your objective. In HR an example would be sending an e-mail out to announce that you are conducting a live meeting and also providing a taped version of the meeting. Could saying that you will have a taped version available possibly encourage employees not to attend the live meeting? What effect would this have on you achieving your communication objectives? If this is a concern, then you may want to consider both how you communicate these media (eg together or separate) and whether you want to offer them both.

Conclusion

According to Dieter Rams, the famous German designer behind Braun's most innovative products and inspiration to Apple's Chief Design Officer Jony Ive, 'Good design is making something intelligible and memorable. Great design is making something memorable and meaningful'. That is exactly what we want and need to do in our communication campaigns, selecting and designing the media which will make our messages both memorable and meaningful to our various audiences. We need to take the time to do what designers do best, which is designing not necessarily what is best practice but is the best or 'right' fit for our organization. We want to achieve the wow factor, as described by Vicky Edwards, which will ensure that the time, money and energy we use in developing our media are creating the desired impact and behaviours. Also, as explained throughout the chapter, by understanding how each medium will work individually and together, we can get the right mix so that our media work effectively to engage and create the desired calls to action. By getting all of this right we can effectively deliver against the objectives we developed in the last chapter.

Top tips on medium

- Select medium/media that have the right 'fit' for your organization and communications campaign – aligning to your objectives, your culture, your audience and your timelines.
- Understand the advantages of each medium, selecting those where the benefits and costs will meet the needs of your communications campaign.
- Ensure that you have taken into consideration what each medium can and cannot achieve, and how this fits into your overall objectives and calls to action.
- Understand how the ever-increasing use of digital media will or will not work at your organization, using those that work best with your organization from a culture and technology perspective.

Skills for being an effective designer

- Ability to bring ideas and designs to the table that are relevant and take into consideration the objectives of the communications campaign.
- Ability to select and bring together the right variety of media to appeal to and engage with the needs of the different audiences.
- Ability to design and develop media that will leave an imprint on your audience.
- Understanding of the value of each medium, and how they will work effectively in an organization.
- Understanding of the latest trends and their role within an organization's communications campaign.

References

CIPD (2010) *Harnessing the power of employee communications*, September, http://www.cipd.co.uk/hr-resources/research/employee-communication-power.aspx

CIPD (2013) *Social Technology, Social Business?* December, http://www.cipd.co.uk/hr-resources/survey-reports/social-technology-business.aspx [accessed 2 October 2015]

Deloitte (2014) *Mobile ConsumerSurvey*, http://www2.deloitte.com/uk/en/pages/technology-media-and-telecommunications/articles/mobile-consumer-survey-2014.html

The Disney Institute Blog (2014) https://disneyinstitute.com/blog/2014/03/leadership-lessons-from-walt-disney-how-to-inspire-your-team/252/, March [accessed 2 October 2015]

Ofcom (2014) *UK Adults' Media and Attitudes* report, http://stakeholders.ofcom.org.uk/market-data-research/other/research-publications/adults/adults-media-lit-14/

Oxford English Dictionary Online, www.oed.com

Wikipedia, https://en.wikipedia.org/wiki/Conversation [accessed 2 October 2015]

WorldatWork (2015) *Trends in Employee Recognition Survey*, https://www.worldatwork.org/adimLink?id=78679 [accessed 2 October 2015]

PLANNING

Planning

03

Introduction

According to Sir John Harvey-Jones, a famous English businessman and television presenter: 'Planning is an unnatural process, it is much more fun to do something'. Does this quote sound familiar, have you or someone on your team questioned or challenged the reason for spending the time and energy to plan for a communications campaign? Would you prefer just getting on and doing it? Well, let me share with you the rest of Sir John Harvey-Jones's quote: 'And the nicest thing about not planning is that failure comes as a complete surprise rather than being preceded by a period of worry and depression'. So yes, by not planning we do not have some of the challenges and emotions linked to the planning process, but the odds are also good that we will fail. I don't know about you, but I'd much prefer succeeding, even if it involves a bit more work.

I'd like you to wear the hat of a *project manager* in this chapter. This is an obvious hat to wear when discussing planning, as project managers are the ones you bring in and think of when you want a project to be managed in an effective manner. I've been lucky enough over the years to have some amazing project managers alongside me on key projects, and they have been the difference between success and failure. According to Andrew Jeffries, an experienced project manager who is currently the manager of a programme to design and build a new £200 million polar research ship for the British Antarctic Survey: 'Your role can be described as ensuring a successful outcome and a journey to that outcome which is under control'. To me the 'under control' is the key to effective project management. It's up to you to control the communications campaign, making sure that at any point in time throughout the campaign you and your team have a clear understanding (and agreement) as to what needs to be done, by whom and by when. Without this clarity you risk making mistakes, duplicating efforts, and other actions which can negatively impact the success of your communications campaign.

In this chapter we will cover the following:

- Why plan?
- How to plan.

Why plan?

To answer this question let me first share with you a real-life example of what happened when a project was not properly planned and managed. The construction of the Scottish Parliament building in 2004 overran initial costs by a factor of 10 and was delayed by three years, and is used in the project management world as an example of project failure (*Supply Management*, 2004).

What led to this were factors such as the design not being agreed before the project began, the project manager resigning just over a year into the project, and the unexpected deaths of the lead sponsor and architect. The deaths were unfortunate and certainly could not have been planned for, but the design not being agreed was definitely something from a planning perspective that should have been agreed before they began construction. In the HR world it would be like rolling out a new performance management system without identifying what elements of performance are to be assessed and evaluated. Or putting in place a new bonus scheme when we hadn't yet decided what actions/behaviours we were rewarding. We would never do that, right? Regarding the project manager resigning, it was cited that he left due to the tension between the project sponsor and the architect. This is understandable as it's written that the architect added 4,000 square metres (+14 per cent) to the design. I'm not blaming the architect (or the project sponsor); I'm just saying that this could possibly have been prevented if agreements had been made prior to the project kicking off. I know, easy for me to say, I wasn't involved!

As we luckily won't be asked to build a government building, but a human resources communications campaign, Figure 3.1 provides some more practical explanations as to why it is important to plan.

Let's discuss each of these individually.

FIGURE 3.1 The importance of planning

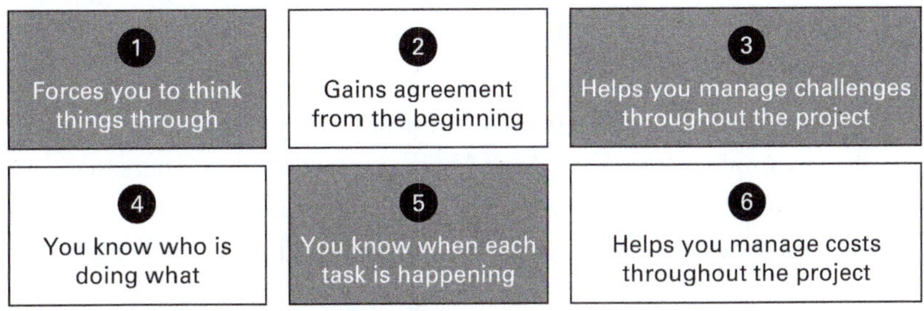

1. Forces you to think things through

Have you ever been in a situation where you finished something and thought: I wish I had thought of that sooner? Once when I was leading a communications campaign, the team came up with a great idea to create a video to explain each of our fantastic company benefits. We thought this would be great, as each location could share it with their teams both at launch and as new employees joined the company. We put a lot of time and energy into creating the video, and got great feedback from business partners along the way. We finalized the video and sent it to all of our UK locations.

So how was it received? Well, the feedback was that they thought it looked great, but as their computers were not set up to have sound, they couldn't hear what was being said. Ouch, did we make a big mistake or what? If only we had thought things through and spoken to the right people, we would have known that videos were not an effective communications vehicle. Luckily we developed the video in-house so we didn't waste the company's money (except for purchasing the CDs and posting them), but we did waste our time and energy. If we had discussed this as we planned the project we could have either eliminated the idea of a video or found a way for locations to allow sound on their computers.

2. Gains agreement from the beginning

For this point I will go back to the Scottish Parliament example. Remember how they had not finalized the design before the project began? Well, because of this a huge amount of time (three years) and money (an increase of initial costs by 10 per cent) were lost. I don't know about you, but in the companies where I've worked it would not be acceptable to lose this amount of time and money.

Gaining agreement is key, but just as key is gaining agreement from the right people. It is important to ask yourself a few questions:

- Who needs to approve it from a *governance* perspective? For example, is there an approval chain that needs to be respected? If there is not a formal approval chain at your company, I suggest that you go to your manager and ask them who they believe needs to provide agreement.
- Who should approve it from a *business buy-in* perspective? For example, is there someone (or even more than one person) in the business that you need on your side in order for the communications campaign to be a success? What risk will there

be if they are not on your side, eg could they cause you problems throughout your campaign?

- Who should approve it from an *input* perspective? For example, is there someone in the business or from another function that could provide valuable input which is required before gaining agreement on the project plan? Going back to the situation I explained previously with the video, was there someone we could have gone to for agreement of the plan who would have highlighted that the video would not work for the business?

3. Helps you manage challenges throughout the project

Although I'd love to say that all projects I've led have had no challenges, surprises etc, unfortunately that would not be true. Every project, no matter how well planned, will have challenges; that's just reality. Our job is to have a plan in place so that we can deal quickly and effectively with these challenges. Without a plan we cannot do this, and challenges could derail our project, making it impossible to go forward.

Going back to the video situation, the bad news was that the video did not work as a communication vehicle at our locations as the computers had no sound. The good news was that our project team quickly came up with a Plan B. This time we ensured that we included the right people in the decision making, and decided to create and distribute an information pack to all locations. We also decided together that the video would have some use in some of the larger locations where there were training rooms which had computers with sound. We were able to overcome the challenge, replacing one aspect of our communications campaign with another one, and even found a way to use the video.

4. You know who is doing what

It may be obvious that in a communications campaign you should know who is doing what, but I've been involved in projects where this hasn't happened. What this does is cause confusion, frustration, duplication and a variety of other challenges. If through your project planning you don't clearly spell out who has responsibility for each action, you are setting your team and your communications campaign up to fail.

In addition to knowing *who is doing what*, it is just as critical to identify *what they are doing* (eg their role for the task). A very helpful tool for doing this is a Six Sigma tool called a RACI, which is a responsibility assignment matrix. A RACI helps you identify roles and responsibilities so that you avoid confusion during the campaign, setting expectations of people involved in your project from the beginning. The acronym RACI stands for:

- R = Responsible: the person who does the work to achieve the task. They have responsibility for getting the work done or ensuring that decisions are made. There is normally only one person who is responsible for a task.
- A = Accountable: the person who is accountable for the correct and thorough completion of the task. They are often the project sponsor. Think of this person as the one everyone comes to if something doesn't happen properly in the project.
- C = Consulted: the people who provide information for the project, and are consulted throughout.
- I = Informed: the people who are kept informed throughout the project. This is done as they need to know what is going on and/or are affected by the outcome.

A RACI matrix can be created in table format in either Word or Excel (I personally prefer Excel as you can more easily sort the information). There are detailed books on how to create the RACI matrix, but to illustrate the concept I've provided you with a high-level summary of the key steps and an example. I've used the situation with the video as the example, and for this scenario I've made the assumption that we have already gained agreement to develop the video. Here are the steps to follow:

1. The first step is to create the vertical rows of your matrix. To do this you should list all of the key tasks and appropriate sub-tasks from your detailed communications campaign project plan (Table 3.1). I would suggest and challenge you to include only those that require the RACI exercise, avoiding any generic activities such as attending meetings. Another suggestion is to describe each task/sub-task using an action verb. When the action requires a decision, use words that indicate the primary outcome.
2. The second step is to create the horizontal columns for your matrix. To do this you should identify and list the various people that will have a role in completing these tasks (Table 3.2). It is often better to list too many people at this stage, for if you find that they do not have a role, then you can remove them from the list at a later date.

TABLE 3.1 RACI matrix: key tasks

Task: Develop video
1. Write script
2. Develop graphics
3. Select music
4. Gain approval on script, graphics and music
5. Select actors
6. Select location and time
7. Film and edit video
8. Gain final approval on video

TABLE 3.2 RACI matrix: list of key individuals

Task: Develop video	HR	IT	Finance	Marketing	Business Partner
1. Write script					
2. Develop graphics					
3. Select music					
4. Gain approval on script, graphics and music					
5. Select actors					
6. Select location and time					
7. Film and edit video					
8. Gain final approval on video					

TABLE 3.3 RACI matrix: assignment of roles

Task: Develop video	HR	IT	Marketing	Business Partner	Project Sponsor
1. Write script	R		C	C	A
2. Develop graphics	C	I	R	C	A
3. Select music	C		R		A
4. Gain approval on script, graphics and music	R	C	I	C	A
5. Select actors	R		C	C	A
6. Select location and time	I	I	R	I	A
7. Film and edit video	I	R	I	I	A
8. Gain final approval on video					

3 The third step, which is often quite challenging and generates many debates, is to assign each person one of the RACI roles (Table 3.3). For example, who will be the one person responsible (R) for completing the task? Will others be involved, but only consulted? If so, when do they need to be consulted? Use the RACI matrix to clearly agree and spell this out at the beginning of your campaign. *Note*: You will notice that I have removed the finance column from the RACI table. This was done as there were no tasks which this individual had a role to play in respect to developing the video.

4 The fourth step is to conduct the vertical and horizontal analysis to see if the matrix is balanced. Some things to ask yourself are:

- Does each task/sub-task have all roles assigned?
- Does one person(s) have too many roles, which could possibly slow down and/or hold up the project? If they do, you may want to consider having someone else from that function join the project/campaign.

- Are there too many Cs? If there are, you may find that this will slow down the project. Ask yourself, does this person really need to be consulted?

5 The final step is to share the RACI matrix with the entire project team. As stated at the beginning of this section, you want to know who is doing what, and for this to be clear to everyone who has a role to play.

5. You know when each task is happening

Another helpful feature about project planning is that it forces you to map out when each task will need to be completed. Without this I've seen deadlines slip or not be achieved, as well as confusion between the various project members.

Let's use the video example again to illustrate this point. We'll use the tasks and sub-tasks listed in the RACI. The first thing to do when assigning timelines is to start at the end. In this example it is when you need to distribute the video, which for illustrative purposes is 15 September. Working backwards from this date you assign timelines for each of the sub-tasks. I suggest that you make sure you give yourself ample time to complete each task, and think about the interdependencies. Table 3.4 shows how it will look.

TABLE 3.4 RACI matrix: assignment of timelines

Task: Develop video	Timeline
1. Write script	1–30 June
2. Develop graphics	1–30 July
3. Select music	1–30 July
4. Gain approval on script, music and graphics	31 July
5. Select actors	1–31 July
6. Select location and time	15–31 July
7. Film and edit video	1–30 August
8. Gain final approval on video	1 September

As you can see in this example, by creating and using your project plan you can ensure that you know when each task is happening.

6. Helps you manage costs

This last reason is one that is always important at any organization, which is about managing costs. I've already cited the cost impact for the failures in the construction of the Scottish Parliament building, but have you also heard about the project failures for the construction of the Sydney Opera House (*Architecture and Design*, 2013)? The original estimate was a cost of A $7 million, but because of the bad project management and significant delays it ended up costing over A $100 million.

In relation to HR and communication campaigns, if they are not planned for properly, costs will definitely increase. I've seen this in a variety of ways, whether it be direct costs such as consultant fees, or indirect costs such as increased time commitments from you and your team. Either way, as costs are always closely reviewed at any organization, we definitely want to manage them properly.

I experienced this first-hand when my organization was relaunching one of its HR programmes. The project team had agreed the objectives of the project, agreed responsibilities and also agreed timelines. We also agreed that we would hire a communications consultant to help us with designs for the communications campaign. A few of us met with the consultant, explained what we wanted, and sent them on their way to develop design proposals. However, what we had not included in our plan was a step which involved gaining agreement from the full team on the concepts of the designs. What this meant was that when the designs came back they did not meet the approval of the full team, and we had to have them redone. As consultants charge by the hour this meant an increase in their fees, and the ultimate cost of the communications campaign. Had we planned more effectively we would have been able to manage costs better.

How to plan

In the first part of this chapter I've explained why it is important to plan. In the second part of this chapter we will move on to how to plan. To introduce you to the world of project managing I'm dividing it into four stages (Figure 3.2).

For each of these stages I will be providing information so that you understand the concepts, and can adjust and/or adapt them for your communications

FIGURE 3.2 The stages of planning

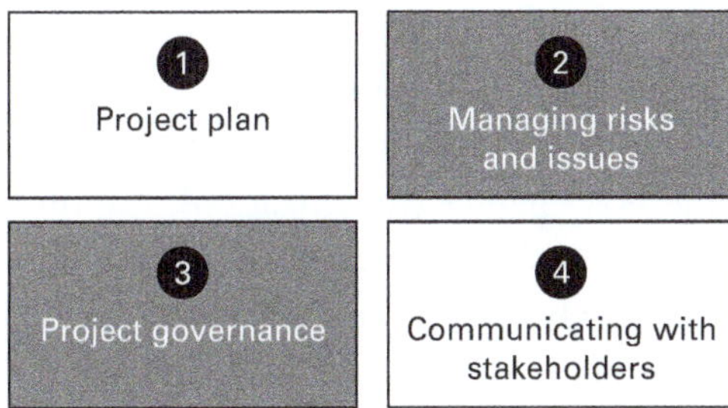

campaign and your organization. This will be helpful to you if you have to do the planning yourself, or even if you are lucky enough to have a project planner.

1. Project plan

Project planning, as explained at the start of this chapter, allows you to have control over your communications campaign. It does this by managing the activities, resources and timelines to achieve your specific goals, and does so through a project plan. Depending on the project management method or tool, there are various ways to map it out. In my aim to make this book HR-friendly, I am going to consolidate them into the key headings outlined in Figure 3.3.

To illustrate this approach I'm going to use *preparing a family meal* as the project. The reason I've selected this is that it is a great example of how even having a fantastic chef doesn't necessarily ensure that the meal will run smoothly, and also because it is something which we can all easily understand.

Objectives/outcomes

One of the biggest reasons a project can fail is through confusion and/or mismatched expectations. Using our example, what happens if the guests

FIGURE 3.3 Developing the project plan

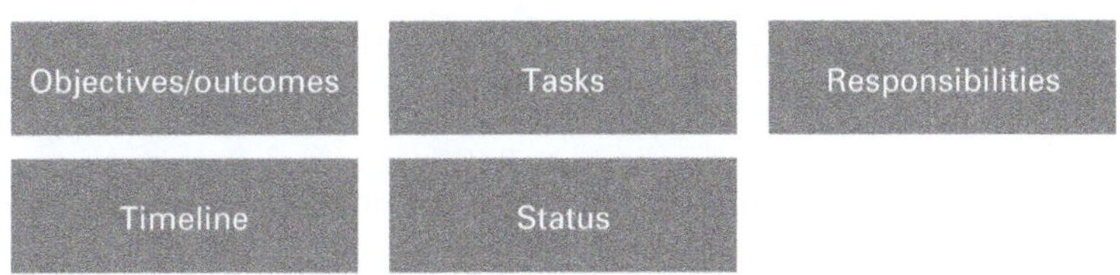

have expectations for a traditional roast dinner, and you decide to be a bit different and serve a beef wellington? Whilst it may be a lovely meal, your guests arrived expecting something very different from what was put in front of them, and may or may not be happy.

The good news about objectives is that we have already addressed and created them in the first chapter (Investigation). Capture these objectives on your project plan, first checking that your project sponsor and project team are in agreement. My suggestion is to put them at the front of your project plan so that this is the first thing documented and appearing in the project plan. This is helpful not only to clarify expectations, but to ensure that the team doesn't stray from them, bringing you back to this agreed set of principles.

The other part of this step relates to outcomes. You need to be very clear in your project plan on exactly what the project is about and what you are trying to achieve. How will you measure success, and what are your critical success factors?

Here is an example using the family meal:

Objectives: To prepare a meal to feed your family of 20 to be on the table at 4.00 pm.

Outcomes: The food is served in the right order and at the right temperature (eg everything that is to be served warm is warm and not cold).
You have enough food for everyone.
Everyone enjoys themselves and tells you how much they have enjoyed the meal.

Tasks

Tasks can be defined as the various actions or activities which need to take place in order to complete your project. Personally I am not a big fan of task lists which are overly complex or long, as my project teams (and I) end up not using them. Also, the more complex/long a project plan is, the more time it takes and the harder it is to maintain and update. It is important to plan at the appropriate level of detail, using only those that are purposeful and actionable.

One technique I've seen and used is to break your project tasks into stages, each representing different areas or sections of the project. This helps make it a bit more manageable. Examples of sections using our family meal example could be: Planning – Food Preparation – Cooking – Table Setting – Serving.

For an HR communications campaign it could be similar to the one shown in Table 3.5.

TABLE 3.5 Project stages

Section	Tasks associated with
Planning	Conducting investigation, setting objectives, assigning roles & responsibilities (preparing RACI), and agreeing deliverables and timeline.
Development	Developing the various communication material and medium.
Systems	Developing systems (eg intranet, apps) where applicable.
Rollout	Activities directly linked to rollout (eg send out e-mail, invite employees to kick off party).
Testing	Testing impact of campaign before, during and after launch.

To further illustrate how to create tasks, I've listed below some guidelines which may help using our family meal example:

- Document the dishes and then break each dish down into the key tasks which are needed in order to prepare.
- Work backwards from the time you wish to serve the dish.
- Think about how many dishes you can work on at one time, thinking about space and equipment (eg oven, hob).
- Think about how many dishes can be cooked at the same time (eg temperature).

Based on these guidelines, Table 3.6 shows how your sub-tasks may look for the task of preparing the turkey.

As you can see, each of the individual sub-tasks is broken down to show all of the work which is required in order to serve the turkey at your family meal.

Responsibilities

Once you've created your task and sub-task list, the next step is to assign responsibilities. As explained earlier in the chapter, this is critical so that it is clear who is doing what. If you are using a RACI, you would list the person who has been assigned the 'R'. If you are not using a RACI, either because you feel it is not necessary or you have another tool, that's fine; just make

TABLE 3.6 Example of task and sub-tasks

Task: Prepare turkey
1. Take turkey out of fridge to thaw.
2. Preheat oven.
3. Rinse and dry turkey.
4. Chop vegetables to put in turkey cavity.
5. Measure oils & spices for mix.
6. Stuff turkey cavity with vegetables.
7. Apply mix to outside of turkey.
8. Put turkey in oven.
9. Take turkey out of oven and let it rest.
10. Carve turkey.

sure that in your project plan you list who is ultimately responsible for ensuring that the task has been completed.

Using our family dinner example and the tasks shown in the previous section, Table 3.7 provides an example of assigning responsibilities. You will notice that I have not used a RACI. This is because this project is fairly straightforward, and thus a RACI would not be necessary.

Another key benefit of assigning responsibilities is to make sure that the person performing the task is available and prepared at the right time. Think about it: if Uncle Bob, who has responsibility for carving the turkey, is outside playing football with the kids in the garden or taking a nap after the football match, he won't be able to carve the turkey. By clearly assigning responsibilities everyone knows exactly which tasks they will be held responsible for, and will have made the time to do so.

Timeline

Picture your family dinner, with all of your family members sitting around your table eager and ready to enjoy your lovely meal. Now picture them

TABLE 3.7 Responsibilities for sub-tasks

Task: Prepare turkey	Responsibilities
1. Take turkey out of fridge to thaw.	Dad
2. Rinse and dry turkey.	Mum
3. Chop vegetables to put in turkey cavity.	Daughter Chloe
4. Measure oils & spices for mix.	Daughter Chloe
5. Stuff turkey cavity with vegetables.	Daughter Chloe
6. Apply mix to outside of turkey.	Mum
7. Preheat oven.	Daughter Chloe
8. Put turkey in oven.	Mum
9. Take turkey out of oven and let it rest.	Dad
10. Carve turkey.	Uncle Bob

sitting bored, frustrated and/or disappointed as the food isn't ready, is cold and/or comes out at different times. You certainly wouldn't allow this at a restaurant, and your family members, although a lot more patient, won't appreciate this happening at your dinner.

A timeline helps you plan out the tasks in advance so that they happen in the right sequence. They do so by communicating to you and your project team the key milestones which need to be achieved by what timescale.

Here are some guidelines on how to set timelines:

- *Set realistic timelines*: It is no use setting timelines if no one is going to be able to achieve these. Make sure that each timeline is realistic to both the project and the person responsible for achieving the task.
- *Set timelines based on interdependencies*: It is important to think of the interdependencies up-front, and address them. For example, if the turkey can't be put in the oven until the oven is warm, set the timeline for turning on the oven before the timeline for cooking the turkey.

- *Review your timelines frequently*: It is critical to set your timelines and go back to them numerous times throughout your campaign. This ensures that nothing has changed which will impact the completion of each task.
- *Adjust timelines if necessary*: As you review your timelines you should adjust them if necessary. I know that sometimes you don't want to admit that something cannot be achieved, but it is better to adjust than to fail, right?

In the example in Table 3.8 I have added timelines to each sub-task using the guidelines above. In developing the timelines I've worked backwards from a serving time of 4.00 pm. Poor Dad has to wake up at 5.00 am to thaw the turkey, but at least he can go back to sleep and leave Mum and daughter Chloe to do most of the preparation. You'll also see that Mum and Chloe have shared the responsibilities so that they can work more efficiently. Finally, Dad jumps in again at the end to take out the turkey, so that Mum and Chloe can finish the other tasks (thanks Dad!).

TABLE 3.8 Timelines for sub-tasks

Task. Prepare turkey	Responsibilities	Timeline
1. Take turkey out of fridge to thaw.	Dad	5.00 am
2. Rinse and dry turkey.	Mum	8.00 am
3. Chop vegetables to put in turkey cavity.	Daughter Chloe	8.00 am
4. Measure oils & spices for mix.	Daughter Chloe	8.30 am
5. Stuff turkey cavity with vegetables.	Daughter Chloe	9.00 am
6. Apply mix to outside of turkey.	Mum	9.30 am
7. Preheat oven.	Daughter Chloe	9.30 am
8. Put turkey in oven.	Mum	10.00 am
9. Take turkey out of oven and let it rest.	Dad	3.30 pm
10. Carve turkey.	Uncle Bob	3.45 pm

Status

As I've mentioned a few times, project planning and management involves keeping your communications campaign under control. The best way to describe the status section of a project plan is that it explains the 'health' of a specific task, which feeds into the overall health of the communications campaign. Reporting on the status of tasks can help as follows:

- *Keeps your project sponsor and team fully informed:* Have you ever been in a car ride with your children (or someone else's children) when they ask you over and over again 'are we there yet?' They do this not to annoy you, but because they want an updated status report on when they are going to get to their destination. Now I'm not saying that your project team are children, but they still do need to know what is going on, and when they will get to the various communication campaign 'destinations'. By providing status updates, you are answering the 'are we there yet' question as well as others throughout the communications campaign.

  It is just as important to keep your project sponsor informed. This is the person that others come to with questions, so it is important that they are armed with information and answers to respond accordingly.
- *Creates clarity from confusion and/or mistakes*: Clarity, which can be defined quite simply as being clear, is critical to ensure the success of your communications campaign. By providing status updates to your team you ensure that everyone is clear as to their role, the timelines etc which will prevent confusion and/or mistakes throughout your communications campaign.
- *Identifies any potential changes which may need to be made*: As covered already in this chapter, it is important to be flexible throughout your communications campaign, adjusting timelines, tasks etc as required. By providing status updates you are able to recognize if/when these need to occur.
- *Identifies any potential risks to the project/campaign*: Risks, as we will discuss in more detail in the next section, are extremely critical to manage in your communications campaign. Creating and updating statuses throughout your project will assist you in identifying and managing these important risks.

- *Acts as a way to engage your team*: As you know, keeping people engaged throughout a project can be challenging. One way to do this is by providing and communicating statuses, thus pulling them back into the project, and ensuring that they are adequately engaged.
- *Provides a mechanism for celebrating successes*: I am a huge fan of celebrating successes, especially during somewhat lengthy communication campaigns where we all need a bit of fun. By providing status updates you are given a mechanism to celebrate these key successes along the way.

Here are some guidelines on how to manage the status of a project plan:

- make them concise and crisp so they can be read and absorbed quickly;
- include specific details where relevant (eg percentage completed, planned completion etc);
- include information on any risks or obstacles.

Some people like to colour-code status updates to make them visually appealing. One approach to use with colour-coding is: green = complete, yellow = on track for completion, red = risk for completion. Keep in mind that not everyone can see colours, so don't rely solely on colours for your updates.

In the example in Table 3.9 I have added the status for each sub-task using the above guidelines.

This example is a bit simplistic. In this situation you probably wouldn't spend the time writing the status, but merely tick the boxes when the tasks are complete. However, in a more complex communications campaign when the project takes a longer amount of time and more people are involved, it is important to add and update statuses throughout the project. Another side benefit of this is that it gives team members the push they need to complete the task. When they know that during each project team meeting any open tasks will be read out, they don't want their name to be next to tasks which appear outstanding and/or a risk.

2. Managing risks and issues

Remember when I discussed the importance of managing the 'health' of a project/campaign? Well, managing risk and issues is all about ensuring

TABLE 3.9 Status of sub-task completion

Task. Prepare turkey	Responsibilities	Timeline	Status
1. Take turkey out of fridge to thaw.	Dad	5.00 am	Complete
2. Rinse and dry turkey.	Mum	8.00 am	Complete
3. Chop vegetables to put in turkey cavity.	Daughter Chloe	8.00 am	Complete
4. Measure oils & spices for mix.	Daughter Chloe	8.30 am	Delayed as Chloe is still chopping vegetables.
5. Stuff turkey cavity with vegetables.	Daughter Chloe	9.00 am	
6. Apply mix to outside of turkey.	Mum	9.30 am	
7. Preheat oven.	Daughter Chloe	9.30 am	
8. Put turkey in oven.	Mum	10.00 am	
9. Take turkey out of oven and let it rest.	Dad	3.30 pm	On track, as Dad has an alarm set
10. Carve turkey.	Uncle Bob	3.45 pm	A bit of a risk as Uncle Bob is signed up for family football game. Plan B is having Dad carve the turkey.

that your communications campaign is healthy and/or treated properly for 'illnesses' along the way. By managing these you minimize the impact of project threats, and react and seize opportunities that occur. Benjamin Disraeli, the 19th-century prime minister of the UK, once said: 'What we anticipate seldom occurs, what we least expected generally happens'. By project managing we are able to do just this: anticipate and manage these risks and issues.

This will allow you to deliver your campaign on time, on budget and meeting the overall objectives. Also, you and your team will be much happier as you won't end up in 'fire-fighting' mode, which means reacting to problems and/or failures which could have been prevented.

Before I go any further on this topic, I thought it important to provide definitions of both words. A 'risk' is something that could go wrong, and an 'issue' is something that has gone wrong. The key with project planning is to have contingency plans to manage both of these: both what can or will occur. Here are a few suggestions on how to manage risks and issues.

Build a way to identify and report

A common way of doing this is to create a separate tab in your project plan to be called 'Risk & Issue Register'. By doing this you will ensure that they are captured and addressed throughout your communications campaign. A suggestion is to formally refer to and address the register during each project team meeting.

Identify them early

It is important to raise these risks and issues as soon as you know of them. That way it gives you and the team more of an opportunity to resolve the matters.

Assign responsibilities

As you'll see in Table 3.10 below, you need to assign responsibility to who will handle the plan for each risk or issue. By doing this, the person will be prepared to handle it up-front and/or if the issue occurs.

Consider both threats and opportunities

Not all risks are negative; sometimes you can find an opportunity in them. Using our family meal example, the risk was that Uncle Bob may not be able to carve the turkey. However, we have already identified a Plan B, which is for Dad to jump in and carve the turkey if Uncle Bob cannot do so.

Analyse and prioritize

What I mean by this is that once you have listed your issues and risks, you should analyse them. Determine if/how they will impact your campaign and what needs to be done to manage them. Prioritize them so that you can action them according to the severity, eg what will impact your campaign the most.

TABLE 3.10 Risk and issues register

Item	Plan	Responsibility
Anthony is a picky eater and may refuse to eat anything.	Have sandwiches prepared and in the refrigerator in case he refuses to eat the meal.	Anthony
A turkey big enough for the entire family may not be available at the local store.	Order the turkey in advance.	Mum
There are lots of courses throughout the meal, and the youngest children may get fidgety.	Have games set up in a different room, and have the oldest prepared to entertain the little ones.	Uncle Bob

Don't be afraid to raise them

This suggestion doesn't appear in any material I've read, but is something I wanted to include as I've seen risks and issues at times be 'swept under the carpet', meaning ignored and/or forgotten. This can cause huge problems. As I've told my teams, it is better to know about something and be able to react than be caught off guard. Going back to the quote at the beginning of this chapter, this will ensure that there are no surprises.

Table 3.10 presents some examples of what you may list in your risk and issue register.

Please note that I've listed only risks in this example, for in a project such as this it is difficult to list any issues. An example of an issue from a communications campaign was the situation where the video was created and computers had no sound for which to play the video. This would have quickly been added to the Risk & Issue Registry, and the team would have determined how best to handle it. As I explained, it was resolved by creating an information pack and using the video in larger locations which had training rooms with sound.

3. Project governance

The governance of a project or communications campaign is what ensures that decisions are made in an effective manner. For example, in the project plan above what would have happened if Chloe had overslept and was not able to perform her tasks? As Mum was the primary chef for the turkey, governance had been informally established that she would jump in, and thus a decision would be quickly made.

The following are some guidelines on how to develop a project governance.

Create a logical and robust approach

It is important to use an approach that works according to how things are done at your company. For example, if your organization has a very formal approach to governance, then everything needs to be very formally documented. If your organization is much more informal, still document your project governance, but do so in a way which will not intimidate or turn off your team members.

Agree and communicate upfront

A project governance structure will not work if it has not been agreed upfront, and has not been communicated. As previously commented, by gaining formal agreement you do not run the risk of someone questioning or challenging decisions which have been made. Also, make sure that the governance is clearly communicated and understood by all team members so that there are no surprises.

Apply throughout project life cycle

Your project governance is not something which should be created and then put on a shelf and ignored. It is something which should be referred to at each step throughout the campaign when decisions need to be made. This will ensure that you are true to what has been agreed.

Using our example, here are some possible governance statements:

- All decisions about major changes to the menu will be made by the project team.
- All decisions about minor changes to the menu or last minute changes in responsibilities will be made by the project lead (Mum).

By creating, agreeing and utilizing a project governance structure/approach you will be able to achieve a positive effect on the quality and speed of decision making on campaign issues. You will also ensure that your campaign is executed in a way to achieve your objectives.

4. Stakeholder communication

This book is all about communication, so it shouldn't be a surprise that I'm mentioning communication in this section about planning. For the same reasons I've talked about the importance of communication to our employees, communicating to our stakeholders is a critical step in the process. This includes our project sponsor, project team and any other stakeholder of the communication campaign. Some reasons for this are as follows:

- *Minimizes misunderstandings and unnecessary delays*: As defined in the introduction, communication is about creating a shared meaning. By communicating with your stakeholders you are ensuring that there is this shared meaning, and thus there are no misunderstandings. By avoiding or minimizing misunderstandings you ensure that the campaign is run more effectively and there are no unnecessary delays.
- *Provides an environment for open and honest contributions by stakeholders*: One of the keys to running an effective team or communications campaign is getting the most out of your contributors, working together to achieve your objectives. By communicating effectively with your stakeholders in an open and honest manner you are creating and providing an environment for their contribution.
- *Ensures there is a focus on completing tasks and identifying any risks and issues*: Creating and managing a project plan is great, but if it is not discussed and used as a communications vehicle with your stakeholders, it will do absolutely nothing. Put simply, you need your stakeholders to make it happen, focusing the team on completing tasks any identifying any risks and/or issues throughout the campaign.
- *Sets you and the team up for success*: Your ultimate goal is to achieve your objectives and success for the communications campaign. By communicating to and working with your stakeholders you are setting the project and the team up for success, ensuring that everyone is clear about roles, expectations, timelines etc.

The following are some suggestions on how to communicate with your stakeholders.

Agree on how and when you will communicate

It is important to agree with your team how you will communicate with each other throughout the campaign. As you know, not everyone communicates and absorbs information in the same way, so it is important to work with your project team to find a way(s) that will make your team effective. For example, do you want weekly update calls? Do you want project minutes sent out? Decide what will work best for you.

Keep messages relevant and on track

As we will cover later when we talk about developing communications content for our employees, it is important to keep your messages relevant to what is being covered. It is easy to stray and go into topics which are outside of topic, but when you are communicating with your very busy stakeholders, try to respect their time and keep everything on track and relevant to what needs to be covered. This will be appreciated by your team, and make you all more efficient.

Create and encourage open and honest communication

Open communication occurs when all parties are able to express and share ideas in conversations and debates. This conversation flow is critical to ensure the success of your campaign, for without it critical pieces of information may not be shared and/or important conversations and debates may not occur. You can achieve this by creating an environment which encourages and recognizes openness and honesty from the start and throughout your campaign.

Aim for achieving win–win solutions

A critical part of working with and communicating with stakeholders is in respect to conflict resolution. Although it may not always be possible, it is advisable to start with a win–win attitude and approach when resolving conflict. This works alongside the previous suggestions of being open and honest, for a win–win approach is built on an environment of trust and partnership. The aim is to not do something 'your way or my way', but to do it in a way which is ultimately the best for the communications campaign.

Good stakeholder management and communication can make a big difference to the success of your communications campaign. It will ensure that you win the support which is necessary for your campaign, and create an effective collaborative and results-oriented environment.

Conclusion

I'd like to end this chapter with another real-life story of planning gone wrong, as it further illustrates the lessons of project planning. Have you ever heard about Operation Sea Lion, which is a part of World War II history? Operation Sea Lion was Germany's planned invasion of the United Kingdom in the autumn of 1940, and (not to ruin the story, but you probably already know) it didn't happen. According to Prime Minister Churchill, the reason it failed was that there was a lack of collaboration in planning and preparing for this endeavour. The chiefs of staff of the German army, navy and air force spent so much time fighting and working at cross purposes that the invasion was repeatedly postponed and finally given up all together.

What we can learn from this example is that if we don't work collaboratively to create and maintain a robust partnership and project plan we will ultimately fail. As I've explained in this chapter we can do this by forming and working effectively with our project team, utilizing project management tools such as RACI, a project plan and a risk and issue register, and continually communicating with our key stakeholders. By doing this we will maintain the control I mentioned at the beginning of this chapter. And by maintaining control we will, as explained in the definition of the word control, be able to influence or direct the course of events. So let's put on our project management hat and get planning!

Top tips on planning

- Have agreed objectives, deliverables and timelines determined and agreed upfront.
- Create a coordinated and collaborative approach to working with your project team and stakeholders.
- Be clear about responsibilities and how decisions are to be made.
- Address and manage tasks, issues and risks honestly and effectively.
- Adopt a flexible and adaptable approach to be able to handle all circumstances.

Skills required to be an effective project manager

- Ability to get things done – be a 'driver'.
- Ability to be flexible, yet firm when necessary.
- Ability to resolve conflict and resolve problems.
- Ability to be a leader – orchestrating activities and challenges.
- Ability to manage relationships.

References

Architecture and Design (2013) Sydney Opera House turns 40 [online] http://www.architectureanddesign.com.au/news/sydney-opera-house-turns-40

Supply Management (2004) The £431 million question, http://www.supplymanagement.com/analysis/features/2004/the-ps431-million-question [accessed 2 October 2015]

LLIES

Allies

04

Introduction

In this chapter we will explore the concept of allies – who they are, why we need them, and how to effectively work with them throughout our communications campaign. This is an integral part of the IMPACT communications model, for as we will discuss later, allies are pivotal and critical to our success.

Before I begin the chapter I'd like to share with you a true story about a sports team. I've selected this story as it illustrates the concepts I'm going to cover in this chapter, showing how getting it right concerning allies can be the difference between winning and losing. The story took place during the 1980 Winter Olympics in Lake Placid, New York in the medal round of the men's ice hockey game between the United States and the Soviet Union. It is referred to as the 'Miracle on Ice' as many say it is one of the greatest upsets in sports history. The Soviet team was the favourite to win not just this game, but the gold medal in the Olympics. This was because they had won the four previous Olympic golds, and their team consisted of experienced professional players who had been playing together for quite a while. The US team on the other hand was made up of amateur and collegiate players, and only one of the 20 players had ever competed at an Olympics. I'm sure you've figured out by now that the United States won, upsetting the Soviet Union and ultimately winning the Olympic gold medal. From my perspective, and keep in mind that I am not an expert on ice hockey, they won for a few key reasons:

- They had a strong leader, bringing in a head coach Herb Brooks, who was an experienced Olympic player before becoming a successful coach. *Note:* As with sports, it is critical to have a strong leader in charge of your communications campaign. This person selects, drives and motivates allies to achieve their objectives.

- He brought in expertise, both with his assistant coach Craig Patrick, with whom he had played in the past, and with Buzz Schneider, who had played previously in the Olympics. *Note*: As explained later, it is important to bring in allies who have strong and varied experience, leveraging their talents throughout the campaign.
- He brought in players who had worked well together in the past, as nine players had played together with Brooks at the University of Minnesota. He brought in another four who had been playing together at Boston University, which was a rival team. This is an interesting one, as some may say that he should not have brought in players from rival teams. But from my perspective I think it worked well, especially in a competitive sport like ice hockey. By leveraging both their teamwork skills and competitiveness they were able to achieve the right balance. *Note*: This shows how getting the right balance of allies is critical in meeting your communication campaign objectives. Think through what will work best in your situation and your campaign.

As you can see through this story, working together with allies as part of a team makes us stronger; working without allies puts us at risk of failing, or losing in this case. I've seen this first-hand in communication campaigns where certain allies were not included and/or not worked with properly. It has been the difference between success and failure, and in hindsight was such an obvious and easy problem to resolve.

In this chapter I'd like you to wear the hat of a *campaigner*. The reason I selected this hat is that when you think of a campaigner you think of someone who is committed to a cause, and achieves it by gaining support from others and working with them throughout the campaign. In this section about allies, that's exactly what we need to do: rally the support of allies to work together to achieve our communication campaign objectives.

In this chapter we will cover the following:

- What is an ally?
- Why do we need allies?
- How to identify and select allies.
- How to work effectively with allies.
- How to work with different types of allies.
- How to work effectively with managers.

What is an ally?

Allies are people who give us advice, information, assistance, backing and even protection as we work together to achieve common objectives. By developing strong relationships with our allies we can get things done more quickly, more smoothly and more effectively. Think of a campaigner who is working for a charity. They can't achieve any of their objectives without allies. They need them to help raise awareness of the charity, money and support in delivering their services. Like these campaigners, our allies are critical to us, and without them we would not be able to develop and deliver our communications campaign effectively.

In this chapter we will use the word 'ally' in the positive sense, meaning that they are in support of our campaign and not attempting to challenge and/or ruin our campaign. As it is our goal to have positive relationships with our allies, I am approaching this discussion in a positive manner.

There are different types of allies:

- *Endorser*: This is a person or persons who will endorse and support your communications campaign, giving it credibility. It could, for example, be the campaign sponsor and/or various business leaders who add their names to the supporter list. They are helpful in showing other business partners and employees a sense of commitment from leaders in the organization. They are also helpful in sharing a perspective that you may not have, as they are often not as close to the project as you and other campaign team members.
- *Partner*: These are people that form your communications campaign project team/group. They work closely together with you to make strategic decisions for the campaign, and to share work responsibilities. They are called partners as they work alongside you throughout the communications campaign, each having different roles based on their area of responsibility and/or expertise.
- *Contributor*: These are people who have an active role in the campaign, but decision making and campaign design are not part of their responsibilities. They do not sit within the project team. Their responsibilities may include tasks such as hosting meetings or conference calls, thus contributing to the overall campaign.
- *External*: These are external people that you bring in to support the communications campaign. They are critical as they bring technical knowledge and/or skills to supplement and support your project team. Examples may be communication consultants, web developers etc.

These are the key categories of what I'd classify as 'formal' allies, and are the categories which I will be covering throughout this chapter. There are other allies which I would classify as 'informal' allies such as employees. They are just as critical to the communications campaign; however, I will not be discussing specifically how to work with them, but focus on these formal allies. Nevertheless, much of what I will say in this chapter is relevant and/or transferable to these informal allies, for people are people, and thus building effective relationships with them will often be achieved in a similar manner.

Why do we need allies?

There are various strong arguments for having allies for your communications campaign. Some of the most compelling reasons are identified in Figure 4.1.

1. Helps you share the workload

As the English proverb goes: 'A problem shared is a problem halved'. This is so true in the business world and in a communications campaign. Think back to the last chapter about planning, and all of the tasks which need to be accomplished in order to achieve your objectives. Being able to share responsibilities decreases your workload by sharing it amongst your very able team. It also expands your resources, giving you more power to reach your targets and achieve your goals.

I experienced this first-hand when I joined a company as an individual contributor, having no team to support me, but being asked to develop and deliver a massive communications campaign. I could have told the business that I couldn't do it, but instead decided to be creative and formed a team from across the business. This proved to be a very wise decision as they were amazing at sharing the workload, and without them I would have never been able to achieve the campaign objectives.

FIGURE 4.1 The benefits of allies

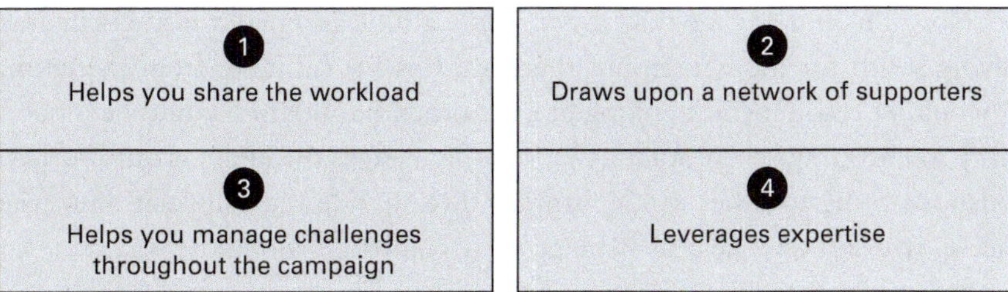

2. Draws upon a network of supporters

According to Winston Churchill: 'There is only one thing worse than fighting with allies, and that is fighting without them'. Your success in your communications campaign relies on supporters, people who will stand up and fight the battle alongside you. The more buy-in you get from your allies at the start and during the campaign, the better chance you will have for them to support you and also bring others with them along the way. It's much better to have a network of supporters than a network of those against your campaign.

Using the example from the previous point, not only were these business partners helpful in getting the work done, but they were also extremely helpful in providing additional support from across the business throughout the campaign. As they came from different parts of the business they were able to rally support and buy-in from across the business in a way that I never could have done on my own.

3. Helps you manage challenges throughout the campaign

When it comes to working your way through the challenges that you face during your communications campaign, it's a great help to be able to draw upon a network of supportive and knowledgeable individuals. Like any project, you know there will be challenges, so you may as well equip yourself with the best people around you to overcome them as they come your way.

Think of a flock of geese flying south before the start of the winter season. If you observe their behaviour, you'll see the geese in the flock working together to achieve the common goal of reaching their winter grounds. They overcome the various challenges of this difficult journey by honking at each other to encourage one another to deal with the challenge of fatigue and motivation. They act as cheerleaders to each other, cheering on those who are getting tired or straggling at the back. They also fly together in a V-formation to deal with the physical challenges of the journey, which helps them deal with fatigue. And finally, they take turns in the 'front bird' position of the V-formation, again working together to deal with the challenge of fatigue.

Now I'm not saying that a communications campaign is the same as flying south for the winter, but there are tips we can take from the geese. I wouldn't recommend honking at each other, but talking would be a good way to encourage each other as we face challenges throughout our journey. Also, working together as a coordinated team, like the V-formation of the geese, will certainly help us manage these challenges along the way.

4. Leverages expertise

Think back to the last chapter about planning, and think of not just the quantity of tasks to be accomplished but the variety of these tasks. By having allies with different knowledge, skills and expertise, you are ensuring that each task can be done effectively and in a timely manner. For example, if you are working with an external web designer to create your intranet, could you have someone from your IT team with first-hand internal design experience work with them instead of you? Not only does this mean less work for you, but they most likely 'talk the same language', and thus are able to move things along more effectively. What about having someone from your internal communications team tasked with writing the newsletter instead of you? Challenge yourself to not only find allies with this expertise, but to utilize them to their fullest.

Another kind of expertise which is helpful to leverage, but not always considered, is your employees. Who better to tell you if the communications are hitting the 'target' and being effective than your employees? I've often gone to a sample of employees with draft material to review, asking them for open and honest feedback, and it has been extremely helpful. One way a company I interviewed did this was by asking employees to volunteer for this role during their pre-campaign survey. By doing this they were not only able to find employees who were willing to help, but also raised awareness that this partnership with employees was happening. This acted as another way to engage employees with the communications material, as they saw that their peers were being involved in the process.

How to identify and select allies

Selecting the 'right' allies is just as important as having allies. As discussed at the start of this chapter, having the wrong ally can cause huge problems, and missing a critical ally can likewise impact your ability to achieve your objectives. Here are some general guidelines for the process of selecting the 'right' allies.

Make a list of allies to approach

Consider the specific skill-sets you require for your communications campaign as well as challenges you may face. Ask yourself which are the key functions that need to be represented (eg finance, IT, communications, procurement) and who could represent this function and best contribute to the campaign. In addition to the skills required, select individuals who:

- are able to speak on behalf of their function;
- have an organized approach to work;
- are able to act as a sounding board, and tell you if you are going in the wrong direction and/or suggest something which will be more effective;
- are able to act as team players.

When making your list of allies, I would suggest including individuals from different functions, at different job levels, of different demographics etc if possible. This ensures that your campaign team is reflective of the organization from a business and an employee perspective. Last but not least, another key individual(s) to include would be someone from the business itself. This does two things: it adds a business perspective, and gives additional credibility to the campaign.

Here's an example from a communications campaign I led to roll out a new benefit. At the last minute we decided to add someone from the business to round out our team. This individual not only brought a unique perspective as they looked at things differently than those of us from support functions, but gave huge credibility to the project. Anytime someone from the business pushed back on what we were doing (which happened frequently in this campaign), I merely used my business partner's name and there was immediate silence. At first I was disappointed that I couldn't achieve this same level of credibility, but in some businesses if you aren't sitting in the business no matter what you do you cannot attain this. Better to face the facts and work with them, right?!

One final note about selecting allies goes back to a point made earlier about individuals who could derail the campaign. Ask yourself these two questions:

- *Will including them in the campaign cause a negative impact?* These are the people that don't have the skills, commitment, time etc to contribute effectively to the campaign. If they don't have what you need, then as difficult as it may be to do, request someone else from their function/demographic group who does.

  An example of this was given in Chapter 1 where the wrong HR business partner was on our project team, and they caused real problems in our communications campaign. In the example the derailer, who was delivering the message directly to employees, turned a positive message into a negative message because they didn't believe in the message. We hadn't spent enough time up-front identifying if they were the right ally. Had we done so we could have either replaced them or convinced them that the message was a positive one. We actually were able to convince them after spending more time with them explaining the message, but unfortunately it was too late. The damage had already been done. So, in conclusion, determine whether this person will have a positive or negative impact on your campaign, and action accordingly.

- *Will not including them in the campaign cause a negative impact?* These are the people that you know from experience will say things negatively about the campaign. You know these people. They say things such as 'if I was involved I would have done it this way', 'I can't believe they did this, I would have done it very differently'. Going back to Churchill's quote about bringing your allies into battle with you, it's better to have them on your side than against you.

  This isn't an HR example, but one which illustrates the point well. I have a son who says he doesn't like curry, any kind of curry. Now I know this isn't true, but I could never convince him of this. So what I do to resolve this is to have him help me prepare the curries, engaging him in the process. By having him be a part of the process all of a sudden the dish is fantastic! Same curry but different approach! Had I not involved him, he wouldn't have eaten the curry, and at the same time he would have negatively impacted others sitting around the table by his complaining. By recognizing his behaviour and acting on it, I was able to turn a negative into a positive.

Have an initial conversation

I know it sounds obvious that you need to have an initial conversation, but often this step is missed because of lack of understanding and/or time. I would suggest organizing a meeting or phone call with your ally and discussing the project with them, balancing sharing information and listening to them. Find out if/how they could contribute to the campaign and what else they are working on. It is critical to check their availability, for even if this individual is fantastic, if they don't have the time to participate, it isn't worth involving them. Lay out the communications campaign, explaining the objectives and timeline, as well as why they would have a stake in it. Talk through ways in which they could be involved and play an important role, and what that would specifically look like.

Based on this conversation, you can decide if they would be a valuable ally for the campaign. The key here is to have this in-depth conversation.

For if it is missed then you may pick the wrong person and/or set the person and the project up for failure based on misunderstandings in respect to expectations.

Secure their endorsement or involvement

Now that you've identified an ally as a potential member of the communications campaign, it is important to go back to them to confirm their endorsement and/or involvement. This is critical, for you do not want to make an assumption that they have formally agreed when in fact they have not done so. In addition, remember to secure approval where applicable from the ally's boss. I've seen situations when the ally agreed and then in the middle of the communications campaign their boss jumped in and said that they could not be involved. My final cautionary note here is to get this in writing. Hopefully it won't happen, but I have seen situations where someone agreed and then forgot they had done so. Unfortunately it ended up as one person's word against another's, which does not lead to good relationships.

Confirm roles and structure

The final guideline is the confirmation of the ally's role in the campaign. I just talked about putting in writing that your ally has agreed to participate, and the next step is to confirm to your ally both their role and the structure of the communications campaign. You need to make it clear so that there are no misunderstandings and/or surprises in the future, setting very clear and concrete expectations. Regarding the role, explain what their role is using the RACI we discussed in Chapter 3 (Planning). Regarding the structure, discuss with them how the campaign will be run in respect to structure of meetings/calls, timelines etc. This not only makes it clear to your ally, but gives you input as to whether the structure will work for all parties involved. As with the previous guideline, after discussing with your ally, put it in writing to confirm what has been agreed.

How to work effectively with allies

Developing alliances will allow you to accomplish the objectives of the communications campaign, and they are key to its success. To assist you with this, here are some suggestions and tips for working effectively with your allies.

Build the relationship first

As I'm sure you know from experience, relationships and partnerships need to be established before any work can be done, at least effectively done. In the next two points I'll explain ways this can be done through gaining respect and trust, but the message here is to make sure that you build these relationships first, before you begin your project/campaign. Some of the most effective teams I've either led or worked on have spent time up-front getting to know each other and building relationships, doing this before the project has even begun. It not only builds a sense of respect and trust, but sends the message to your communications campaign allies that you want to understand and work them now and throughout the project.

An example of this was when I was involved in a global HR project that involved making and then communicating some very sensitive and challenging changes. The person leading this project brought all of us together from around the world, having us come in a day earlier than the work would begin. We spent this day at a spa, getting to know each other in a relaxing and neutral environment. This made a huge difference to the atmosphere and working relationships throughout the meeting, as we had spent time building our relationship and trust first. Had we not done this I'm convinced that we would not have had such a productive meeting, and would definitely not have achieved our objectives.

Now I'm not saying that we always have the time and money to go to a spa together (if only!), but there are other less expensive and timely ways to build relationships. You could add simple and fun ice-breakers to the kick-off meeting, which costs nothing and doesn't add much time either. You could have some coffee/tea and snacks before the meeting, which is low-cost and again doesn't add much time. Get creative, and do what works best for you and in your organization.

Earn their respect

A key aspect of building relationships with allies is to earn and gain their respect. Your allies won't listen and cooperate if they don't respect you, believing that you bring expertise and/or leadership to the campaign, and are the right person to lead it. This doesn't mean that you have to spend hours going on and on about all you know on this topic. This will not only bore your allies, but put them in a defensive position. Instead, find a way to sincerely and effectively show them that you have the knowledge to lead this project. Also, be honest and admit that you are not an expert in every area of the campaign, but instead are wise enough to bring in people such as them, and thus build and leverage the knowledge of others. Finally, provide them with an opportunity to voice their opinions and thoughts, as listening (as I've stated numerous times) is not only critical, but a proven way to achieve respect.

Think back to projects or managers you have worked with and for; haven't you been more effective when you've respected them? Be honest: when you've worked with people you don't respect you don't have the same level of commitment, do you? Take the time up-front to earn the respect of your team, for as the expression goes, it will pay dividends in the end.

Earn their trust

Just as important as earning the respect of allies, is earning their trust. By having the trust of your allies you further your chances of having a true partnership. In addition to partnership it creates a willingness to take risks and enter into the unknown because you trust the other person. This is critical as you face and resolve the challenges that you encounter throughout your communications campaign.

Have common objectives

Now that you have secure working relationships with your communications campaign allies, the next thing to do is to make sure that you have common objectives. Everyone needs to be in complete alignment with what the campaign is tasked with achieving, for if there is misalignment there could be confusion and/or frustration between allies. This needs to be done at the start and during the campaign so that you are all working off the same plan. As suggested in the previous chapter, make the objectives a visible part of the project plan, thus ensuring that these objectives are constantly kept in mind and not forgotten or put away in the bottom drawer.

Think back to the geese flying south for the winter. What would happen if one of the geese didn't understand the objective of flying south and instead started flying north? This would completely disrupt the V-formation, directly impacting their ability to meet their objective. You need to make sure that all 'geese' know exactly what the plan is, taking their assigned place in the formation and thus arriving south in time for winter.

Listen and understand

As an HR professional, I'm sure that listening and understanding comes naturally, as that's what makes you effective in your role. Use these well-developed skills as you work with your allies, making the effort to listen to what they have to say, and thoroughly understand what and how they are contributing.

Think back to the Introduction when I talked about the aim of communicating to achieve a shared meaning. The same is true when communicating with your allies, as this ensures that you both have a common understanding and you both have a similar voice. This also assists in avoiding miscommunications and misunderstanding, which can cause problems throughout your communications campaign.

According to Kim Ewen-Hill, Business Technologist and Innovate Business Systems Owner, CIO at LV= (see case study on p 183): 'It is important to be transparent with your team and invite feedback from start to finish'.

Open your mind to new ideas

One of the lessons I learned early in my career, and I'm almost embarrassed to put it in print, is that I don't have all the answers. I've come to learn and appreciate that the more ideas, the better the solution. Consider ideas from your allies as you'll never know where that next great idea will come from. Don't jump to the conclusion that an idea won't work by rejecting it, but pause, open your mind and consider the possibilities.

An example of this was when I was working on a communications campaign to launch a new online discount programme. A member of the project team was a line manager, who throughout the project brought amazing insight into what a 'normal' employee would want and need. When we were discussing how best to launch the new programme this individual threw out the idea of running lunch-and-learn sessions at our various offices. This wasn't something we had considered as we felt that employees were too busy with their jobs to take the time to come to a session. We had also already decided to have an e-mail, text message and a videoconference, believing that this would work best. These sessions would have been a fourth medium, and the team had agreed that we should only use three. After the team finally finished debating, and decided to listen to our business partner, they quickly convinced all of us that this would work best alongside the other mediums. They were definitely right, as we received fantastic feedback on the sessions. The statistics on enrolment in the scheme also proved our business partner was right, for the data showed that more employees signed up for the scheme where we had been able to conduct these sessions. If we hadn't listened to our business ally, we would have missed this fantastic opportunity to impact the results of our campaign.

Empower your allies

Empowerment is all about sharing the power, giving people permission to contribute, to use their talents to develop ideas and find solutions. Empowering others not only helps in getting things done more effectively, but it creates a positive and effective working environment. This is key when working with allies so that you can get the best contributions from each and every one.

I've already discussed a few ways to empower your allies through concepts such as trust, respect, common objectives and listening. An additional way to do this is by openly sharing information with allies so that they have what they need to contribute. Think back to your geese; if they are all clear as to where they are going they can not only support each other, but jump in and take over should the need arise. Having equally effective allies makes a much stronger team.

How to work with different types of allies

As you know, not all allies are the same. Depending on their role in your communications campaign you will need to work differently with each of them. Based on the four categories of allies which were introduced at the start of the chapter, let's look at how you could work with each category (see Table 4.1).

TABLE 4.1 Working with allies

Category	How to work with them
Endorser	These are the people who endorse and support you, thus it is critical to keep them informed throughout the project. They want and need to know where you are at all times against objectives AND if there are any challenges and risks which arise. They are not going to like surprises, as often others go to them to be the voice of the campaign, so keep them fully informed. You will also want to come to them at key times throughout the project in respect to decision making. As an endorser they may only wish to be approached for key decisions, but it is best to check to see if/when they want to be a part of campaign decisions. My suggestion would be to speak with them up-front to discuss how best to work with them. From my experience many of the endorsers I've worked with do not want to see the full in-depth project plan, but prefer an overview containing the most relevant information. However, it is best not to assume that this is what they want and/or need, so present all options to them, and agree your approach at the start of the campaign.

TABLE 4.1 *Continued*

Category	How to work with them
Partner	These are the people who work alongside you throughout the project, thus it is critical not only to keep them informed throughout the project but to partner with them at each and every step along the way. Use the tools you've developed through the planning process to do this (eg the project plan, the RACI etc), ensuring that they are fully aligned with what is happening throughout the campaign and their role in accomplishing the objectives. Regarding decisions, depending on what has been agreed in the RACI, you should partner with them at the agreed points in time. This is critical as the project and their expectations have been set based on these timelines.
Contributor	These are the people who have less of an active role in the communications campaign, as they contribute at specific times. For this reason you need to ask yourself how much information they require to support the campaign. You need to balance providing too much information, information which is not necessary, with information that is required in order for them to effectively contribute to and support the campaign. This is sometimes called a 'funnel approach', which looks at how much information needs to get through the funnel in order for your allies to be fully informed and thus effective. My suggestion is to think through their role, looking at how and when they are required to contribute. Put yourself in their shoes, and think about what they need to know so that they are effective, and provide this information at the right time and in the right way.
External	Often external contributors are forgotten about during the communications campaign, only going to them when they have a specific role to play. However, this is a mistake, for if you don't involve them throughout the campaign they will not have the information necessary to perform their role and/or will be less effective due to gaps in knowledge. A situation where this may occur is if you used an external vendor to develop a brochure to explain your new HR programme. You could say that they were 'only' creating a brochure, but if they weren't aware of what had happened in other areas of the campaign the brochure may not have been developed in the right way. For example, what happens if you identify through speaking with business partners that employees may not be happy with the new programme as they really liked the previous programme? If the external contributor isn't aware of this they may not include a section in the brochure which shows how the new programme is better than the old programme. Keeping them in the loop will ensure that they have all of the facts and pertinent information to do their job. If they don't have this you are setting them up for failure, and thus doing the same for the campaign. You could also cost your campaign more money, as they may need to redo their work based on lack of understanding.

How to work effectively with managers

I could not finish a chapter talking about allies without talking about managers, and how to work effectively with them. Think back to the start of this chapter when I defined the word ally as someone who gives you advice, information, assistance, backing and protection. Don't many of these words apply to your managers? Aren't they often giving advice, information etc to their employees, whether it be formally or informally? Don't employees go to their manager to seek clarity, advice and even their perspective when messages are communicated? For this reason, managers have a very key role to play in your communications campaign, and should not be forgotten.

Before I give you information on how to work effectively with managers, I first want to address the various roles that managers play in your communications campaign. You'll notice that I'm using the words 'endorser' and 'partner' again, but you will also notice that the definitions for managers are slightly different to those used at the start of this chapter:

- *Endorser*: This category was defined earlier in the chapter as people who will endorse and support your communications campaign, giving it credibility. Managers often play this role, as their employees will go to them for their opinion, asking them to validate the messages. By having your managers educated and on board, you are providing them with the knowledge to be an endorser and supportive of your campaign key messages. If they do not have the necessary information they could actually derail your campaign, as they could act negatively without all of the critical facts and information.
- *Partner*: This category was defined earlier in the chapter as people that form your communications campaign team, sharing responsibilities and working alongside you. This role is slightly different for managers, as often they do not partner until the communications campaign is rolled out. Their role can be direct (delivering the messages directly to employees) and/or indirect (employees coming to them with questions about the messages). Either way, they have an important role as your partner as they are representing the messages and the campaign.

As you can see, managers have multiple roles to play in your communications campaign, often whether they've been asked to or not. That is why it is critical to work effectively with them, so that they are prepared to be effective endorsers and partners. Here are some suggestions and tips for working effectively with your managers, getting the best out of them and what's best for your communications campaign.

Speak to them pre-launch

Picture this: you send out your communications campaign e-mail, text etc and your employees rush in to talk to their manager, and ask them what the messages are all about. And your manager says ... I don't know! I have seen this happen at companies where I've worked, and I'm fairly confident that it will happen at your company if your managers are not involved. For this reason it is important to prepare your managers for these conversations with their employees, doing so pre-launch so that they are armed with the information so that they can support you best.

Brief them fully

Your managers are often the first point of contact for employees and thus they need to be prepared. The best way to prepare them is to fully brief them on the communications campaign prior to it being launched. This includes sharing with them the objectives, the project plan (including timelines) and the key messages. Here are some specific suggestions in respect to the briefing:

- Put yourself in your manager's shoes and ask yourself: 'What would I need to know/see in order to support the campaign?' This helps you develop and deliver exactly what your managers need and not what you think they need.
- Consider developing separate communication material specifically for your managers. The reason for this is that often they may need different information than your employees due to their role in the campaign. This could be speaking notes, FAQs (frequently asked questions) etc. Whatever you give them, make it clear and robust so that they not only have what they need, but also so that all managers are speaking in a consistent manner. Finally, remember to put the development and distribution of this material in your project plan so that it is done in line with your overall campaign timeline.
- Test your manager material before distributing. As discussed with employee communication material, it is helpful to have a test audience to ensure that your desired messages are coming across. I would suggest doing this with a cross-section of managers, eg from those that are fully versed on the topic to those that are completely unaware. This will ensure that your manager material is balanced and comprehensive.

- Consider conducting briefing sessions, either face-to-face, through webinars or sending out packs. Although this adds extra time to your timeline, it can prove to be extremely valuable as it introduces two-way communication to this important step. This further ensures that your managers are fully aware of and versed on the topic and information.

Provide ongoing questions and answers

It is helpful to provide managers with FAQs as part of their briefing material. The point to make here is that it is just as important to update and/or change these questions and answers throughout the communications campaign, or they will no longer meet your managers' needs.

Think about it: if you want your managers to partner effectively, don't they need to have the latest and best information to work from? I know it may be time-consuming and challenging to do this when you are so busy running the campaign, but it is well worth the effort. An example would be if you discover that there is a rumour that only managers can make nominations through the new online recognition scheme. If you don't go back to managers to say that actually employees can nominate co-workers, the message will be incorrect for your employees and the scheme will not be used properly.

Listen and understand

These two words cropped up earlier in the chapter when explaining how to work effectively with allies. They are true again with managers, as your managers are often your 'eyes and ears' throughout your communications campaign. This is because they are able to see first-hand how employees are reacting (eyes) and hear first-hand from their employees what they are saying (ears). If you do not listen to what they have to say through their feedback and/or questions, you will not gain their valuable perspectives and insights. Also, by listening and understanding you will ensure that your managers and the campaign have the all-important shared meaning.

Empower your managers

This was also mentioned previously when talking about working with allies. As with other allies, empowerment is critical to your relationship with your managers, and to the overall campaign. By giving managers the tools and support I've listed on pp 113–14 you will be able to empower them to support their employees and the overall campaign.

By working effectively with your managers you are giving them the tools to support you throughout your communications campaign. They become true advocates and supporters of you and your key messages, ensuring that these are heard and understood by their employees. They can also help you overcome some of the challenges you face in a communications campaign. This is true at St John Ambulance, the UK's leading first aid charity, where they are using their managers effectively as part of their communications strategy. According to Steve Foster, Director of People and Organization at St John Ambulance:

> We have a particular challenge in that our 'workforce', which is a combination of employees and volunteers, is about 20,000 people of whom a couple of thousand work out of our premises. The rest are drivers, trainers and people providing first aid cover at public events. Most of them are volunteers with busy day jobs, which adds to the challenge. As part of our journey to change our communications strategy and approach we are training our managers to use all of the communication tools available to them.

By doing this they are able to leverage the strength and support of their managers, adding them to their team of capable allies.

Conclusion

In this chapter I've shared with you information on why allies are important to have in your communications campaign, and how to work with them effectively. We often think it would be easier to do things on our own, with fewer people involved and fewer questions and challenges. But, as the expression goes, the sum is greater than the parts. Together we are more powerful and more effective.

This is very true in respect to allies, for by joining together we can leverage different knowledge bases and different perspectives, and ultimately set our communications campaign up for success. Put on your 'hat' as a campaigner, doing what they do so well by rallying the support of others to achieve the commitment to the cause they are fighting to promote. If we can achieve this same level of commitment from our allies we will have a better chance of promoting our 'cause', which for us in HR are the messages from our communications campaign.

Top tips on allies

- By working with allies you have more 'power' and can expand your pool of resources.
- Working with allies is a two-way street – they help you and you help them.
- Take the time up-front to develop strong relationships with your allies.
- Clearly define to your allies their role, the timeline, what's in it for them, and set expectations.
- Keep the lines of communication open between you and your allies.
- Don't forget the importance of managers as key allies.

Skills for being an effective campaigner

- Ability to develop and maintain strong working relationships.
- Ability to create and maintain a collaborative work environment.
- Ability to inspire and empower others.
- Ability to compassionately and effectively listen to others.
- Ability to constructively handle conflict and resolve effectively.

CONTENT

Content

05

Introduction

Have you ever heard the term 'stickiness', which is often used by website developers? This is the ultimate goal of any website, as this is what gets your customers to come to your website over and over again. My question to you is: Isn't this what we want from our HR communication material? Don't we want our employees to 'stick' or engage with our communications campaign material? Don't we need this so that our messages are decoded, and employees are clear about their call to action? We can design the most exciting communication media, whether it is a fantastic website, an exciting video or a creative booklet, but if we don't create engaging content we won't get our employees to click, read and/or listen. This is critical, for without this our communications campaign will have failed to meet our objectives.

Did you know that people make judgements within seconds of seeing something? Think of an advertising campaign: which are the ones that capture your attention and which are the ones where you walk away from the television to get something to drink or eat? If you want the first impression of your communication campaign to be a positive one, the key is to have sticky content. If you can create it so that your employees connect and engage with it, and do this quite quickly, then you are more likely to succeed.

In this chapter I'd like you to wear the hat of a *writer*. This is a useful hat to wear when talking about content, as the writer is the one who uses words to express ideas. As Ayn Rand, a Russian-born US novelist said: 'Words are a lens to focus one's mind'. This is exactly what we are trying to do through our content, focusing our employees on the information that we are attempting to share with them.

In this chapter we will cover the following:

- What is content?
- Why is content important?
- Some guiding principles.
- How to create effective content.
- Things to consider.

What is content?

As with media, content has changed over the years, both what it is and how it is used. If I had written this book 10 years ago I would have defined content merely as words and some graphics. However, due to the variety of media we use, as well as techniques that have been developed, content has evolved. Words are still a key driver of content, which is why I have asked you to wear the hat of a writer; however, it also now involves so much more. This includes things such as graphics, web design, video design, and even the use of marketing techniques. Although this gives us a variety to choose from when developing our content, it also gives us more which we need to understand and learn to use effectively.

Why is content important?

To answer this question let me first explain a marketing concept of 'content marketing'. Content marketing is a strategic marketing approach where you focus on creating valuable, relevant and consistent content to attract and retain your audience. The idea is to create informed consumers, ones who will then reward you with business loyalty. Put simply, good content marketing will make a person stop – read – think – and behave differently.

I've included the definition of content marketing as it answers the 'why' question quite well. If we get the content right our employees will, using marketing terms, reward us with business loyalty. In the HR world this may mean increased employee engagement scores, increased participation in an HR scheme, or possibly increased awareness of a business change. Put simply, good communications content will make our employees stop – take notice – take action – engage – and behave differently. Bad communications content will make our employees ignore – take no action – and behave the same. Which would you prefer? Do you want your 'book' to be a best-seller or to sit on the shelves with no one taking notice?

Some guiding principles

The first thing your communications content needs to do is make employees stop and take notice. That shouldn't be hard to do, right? But in a world of information overload it can be quite difficult and challenging. I don't have to explain information overload to you; you experience it every day when you are bombarded with way too many e-mails, texts and messages on social media. Let's face it, there is just too much information for us to process these days. This could cause your employees to skip over, filter out or just ignore your messages. As HR professionals who are trying to communicate effectively, this could additional challenges which we will need to deal with.

One way to overcome these challenges is to keep in mind some guiding principles throughout your communications campaign. I've listed three guiding principles in Table 5.1, although there are many others to choose from. The reason I've selected these is to keep it simple and straightforward for you, but also to align with the definition I gave you previously for the term content marketing, which is to make communications valuable, relevant and consistent.

TABLE 5.1 Content: guiding principles

1. Valuable	The word valuable can be defined as something of great worth. Synonyms include words such as precious, costly and prized. The concept of value is key when developing content, for in order to get your employee's attention you need to show your employees that there is some value to them personally. The acronym WIIFM (what's in it for me?) is another way of looking at the concept of value. Through your content you need to justify to your employees why you are asking them to use their valuable time to pay attention, and what are the benefits of doing this. Ask yourself: how can I show value in my content? Also, what can I do to show this value as quickly as possible so that I make sure that my message is not ignored? One example is by creating an engaging subject header to answer the question WIIFM. You could say: 'Exciting new benefit to help you save money', which could grab your employee's attention as they see the value in saving money. Another more active example would be to say: 'If you want to save money read on'. You decide what words and tone work best for your campaign, but do your best to show the value and show it as quickly as possible.

TABLE 5.1 *Continued*

2.	Relevant	The word relevant can be defined as something which is closely connected or appropriate to the matter at hand. Synonyms include words such as pertinent and applicable. Ask yourself: how many times have you deleted an e-mail without even reading it as you thought it wasn't relevant? As you scroll through your ever-growing inbox, this is a common way to manage the volume. For this reason you need to make sure that as you develop your content you make it relevant to your employees. This may mean that you need to segment your content, meaning you create different content based on what is required and relevant to them.
3.	Consistent	The word consistent can be defined as holding something together. Synonyms include words such as solidity and cohesion. The concept of consistency is key for content as well as all other aspects of the communications campaign. By holding the content together, you are ensuring that employees do not ignore important content as they do not know that it is related to the overall campaign. You can do this by using consistent language, format, colours and branding in your communication campaign. This gives you a better chance of employees recognizing and paying attention to your content. Another benefit of consistency is that it helps build and maintain trust. According to the 2013 *Forum Global Leadership Pulse* survey, lack of consistency can erode trust with employees.

A final point about creating effective communications content is something which Steve Foster, HR Director of People and Organisation, St John Ambulance, shared with me. He pointed out how important it is not to assume that your employees are interested in the same things as you. Now this may sound a bit harsh, as we all want to think that others will be interested in what we have to say, but the fact is that they may not be because they have different priorities. Steve shared with me a story of when one of the global marketing leaders presented on business strategy at an employee meeting at a previous company. An employee raised their hand and asked a question which related to a very local operational issue. The presenter was disappointed that his audience wasn't interested in the strategy and the audience wasn't happy that the presenter wanted to talk global strategy while ignoring an operational problem that might result in job losses. According to Steve: 'The mistake people communicating often make is that they think that everyone has the same interests as them. The reality is that all of us are primarily interested in what impacts us, our team and our place of work.' We need to keep this in mind as we develop and roll out communications, looking at both the content and delivery mechanism through the lens of the audience.

How to create effective content

Now that we have some general guiding principles to consider and follow, the next thing to explore is how we can use these and other more specific principles to achieve effective and engaging content. Going back to writers, this is something which is a key objective for them, for without this their material will not be purchased and/or read.

This section has been broken into two parts to make the information more manageable and meaningful. The first part looks at how to be effective through writing, and the second part looks at how to be effective through graphics. Together they provide a comprehensive set of suggestions of what to consider as you develop the content for your communications campaign.

Through writing

According to US writer EL Doctorow: 'Good writing is supposed to evoke sensation in the reader – not the fact that it is raining, but the feeling of being rained upon'. This quote explains beautifully how we need to use our words not just to recite facts but to change behaviours. To assist you in developing the most effective content through writing, I have put together a very extensive list of 'what you should do' and 'things to avoid'. Together they create a full picture of what you can do to meet your objective of doing what EL Doctorow has said, which is to use words to change behaviours.

Let's start by addressing the ***things you should do***.

1. Think of your employee as a consumer

A consumer can be defined as a person who can make a decision as to whether or not to purchase a product or service. I ask you, in our communication campaigns, isn't that what our employees are? Aren't they the ones who are 'purchasing' what we have to say and what we are asking them to do? For this reason we need to keep this in mind when creating our words, doing our best to think and act like a marketer to use our words to motivate our employees to complete the 'purchase'. A suggestion I'd like to make is something I do often when developing my words, and that is to partner with someone in the marketing department. By asking them either to look at your words or develop them through their marketing lens and/or perspective, you are improving their effectiveness.

2. Put your employee first

Create your words from the employee's perspective, putting yourself in their 'shoes'. Ask yourself: If I were the reader what would I want and need to know? Also, ask yourself: What would I be questioning and/or challenging? Focus the words on providing this key information and answering these questions. Finally, think about what the employee would not be interested in, as this is just as important in order to fully engage them.

3. Keep it simple

Keeping it simple is one of the most common tips from communication experts. A great quote making this point is from John Kotter, a famous lecturer and author. He says: 'Good communication does not mean that you have to speak in perfectly formed sentences and paragraphs. It isn't about slickness. Simple and clear go a long way.'

A common way of describing this concept is by using the famous acronym KISS, which I'm sure we've all heard and/or used before. There are variations of the meaning ranging from 'keep it simple, stupid' to 'keep it short and simple' to 'keep it simple and straightforward'. They all mean the same thing, which is that things work much better if they are kept simple and not complicated. A few suggestions on how to do this are:

- **a** Get rid of words that are redundant, as you are just saying the same thing twice.
- **b** Get rid of too many descriptive words; ask yourself 'is it really necessary'?
- **c** Keep sentences to one idea or point, creating focus and clarity.
- **d** Write sentences which would be comfortable to speak, eg do not run on too long.

4. Write with an active and direct voice

Every communications expert I spoke with stressed the importance of writing with an active and direct voice, and not a passive one. In case you are not familiar with these terms, a sentence written in the active and direct voice is when the person performs the action (the dog bit the postman). In a sentence written in the passive voice the person receives the action (the postman was bitten by the dog). The active sentence is stronger, clearly explaining the action and who did it, showing responsibility. It helps your employees visualize and follow the action. Some tips for doing this are:

- **a** Turn the clause or sentence around by putting the subject first (this was done in the example by moving the word dog to the front of the sentence).
- **b** Change the verb to eliminate the helping verb (this was done in the example by eliminating the word 'was' and just saying 'bit').
- **c** Try not to use 'ing', as it does not work as effectively. For example, instead of saying 'By signing up for this benefit you will save 20 per cent', try saying 'Save £20 when you buy a mobile phone worth £100'. The second phrase is clearer and more action-oriented.

5. Use power words

There are words that are never noticed, and others which stand out, are more persuasive, and have a certain power about them. These, no surprise, are called 'power' words, and bring about an emotional connection or reaction. They should be used as much as possible when developing your content to help engage with your employees. Here are examples of some power words:

Proven	New	Important
Free	Incredible	Fantastic

How did these words make you feel? Did they invoke a reaction? If yes, then use them; if not, then they may not be a power word which will work for you or your communications campaign.

6. Create an engaging subject line

The subject line is the hook that gets your employee to open an e-mail, read a letter, click on a website etc, and thus begin the communications 'journey'. For this reason you need to put your time and creativity into creating something that will be noticed. I have spent hours drafting and testing different subject lines, as I wanted it to be just right. It may be time-consuming, but it is definitely worth the effort.

Here are some suggestions on how to create engaging subject lines:

a Use the word 'you' if possible, as it is one of the best words to grab your employee's attention.

b Use power words to invoke a reaction.

c Use numbers if relevant, as they are eye-catching.

d Finally, keep the subject line short and direct. This is important not only to be engaging, but also so that it can be read quickly.

7. Prioritize messages

Let's face it, communicating HR concepts and programmes is often difficult to do in a concise manner. We often need to communicate a lot of information, and even when we apply concepts such as KISS (as explained above), our messages are still quite lengthy. And what happens with lengthy messages? Our readers drop off, meaning they often stop reading after a certain number of words. For this reason we need to prioritize our messages, ranking them in order of importance.

Pyramid technique

A suggestion from Debi O'Donovan, founder of Reward & Employee Benefits Association, is that you should summarize or headline what the employee needs to know, and then have them either click (for the intranet) or go to another section (for a letter or booklet) if they want to read more. Debi suggests using an approach called the 'pyramid technique'. The best way to explain this technique is to picture your words appearing in a pyramid. You start at the top of the pyramid with a short sentence making your key statement. If the reader doesn't read beyond this sentence they should still have read your most important message. Then you work down the pyramid with your secondary point, then your third point. After this you go on to expand your details about the points above, perhaps with longer sentences. Each time think: 'What if they stopped reading here?', 'Have I summarized all the vital points before going on to add details?' This technique allows you to 'cut from the bottom' if it gets too long. Your last sentences are simply added information and could be removed.

Figure 5.1 illustrates the pyramid technique.

FIGURE 5.1 The pyramid technique

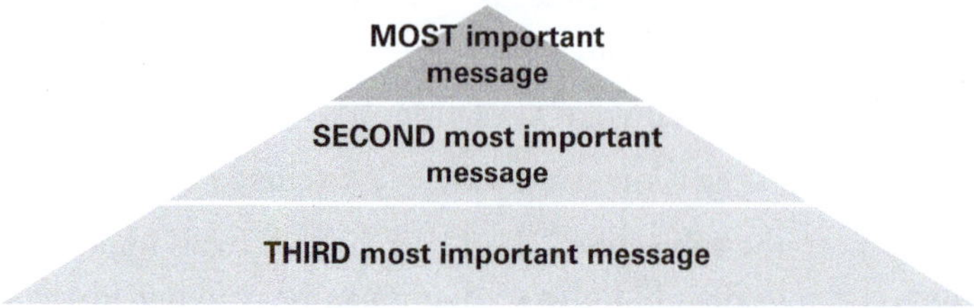

I came across this challenge when we were developing online total reward statements, which is a document which summarizes the various elements of an employee's personal reward package. When testing, we found that employees were clicking on maybe the second or third links to information, but no further than this. Using an expression my teenage children use all the time, they 'couldn't be bothered' to click any further, even if it was to see more information. We resolved this by moving more of the critical information earlier in the messaging so that employees had fewer clicks to make. This follows the pyramid technique which Debi suggested.

8. Personalize content

Few things interest us more than seeing our own name in print or on the screen. Our names are intrinsically tied to our self-perception, and we become more engaged and more trusting of a message if/when our name is shown.

Marketing professionals have been using the technique of personalization for a while now, in fact consumers have grown to expect it. Think of what you receive from your supermarket, coupons that mirror your shopping habits and have your name written on them. How great is that?

In the HR world we are beginning to use this technique thanks to technology, and it has been proven to have positive results. Examples may be to personalize a letter or e-mail to have not only the employee's name, but other details relating to the communications campaign. For example, if you are sending out something explaining changes to a pension scheme, why not include not just their name but also details on how the change will personally impact them? This will engage your employees, making them feel as if the company cares enough to send information specific to only them.

9. Create a call to action

Every communications vehicle should have a call to action, which as explained previously is a response you want your employee to have and take. A few tips on creating a call to action through your words are:

- **a** Use active language so that your employees are clear about what action to take.
- **b** Create a sense of urgency, such as giving a specific deadline, so your employees are clear about the action's timeline.
- **c** Use colour, fonts etc to draw your employees' attention to the action. This is a great way of making the action stand out, looking different to the rest of the content.
- **d** Don't have too many actions. If you have too many it will be confusing and/or distract from your key action(s).

10. Present clear benefits at beginning and ends

People tend to remember what comes first and likewise what comes last. Things in the middle are unfortunately often forgotten. When developing your content, identify these benefits, the WIIFM (what's in it for me?) for the employee. Put these at the beginning of your content and reiterate them again at the end. There is no harm in presenting them twice, for by doing this you have a better chance of achieving your objectives.

Another slightly different way to handle presenting clear benefits is through something called a 'pull-out box'. These are boxes that appear either at the beginning or end of a message, and often list the top three tips, points etc. You will notice that I've done this at the end of each chapter in this book, listing both the top tips and the skills required for each chapter's 'hat'. I've done this to highlight the key points/benefits of the chapter by making it easy and engaging to read these short and direct points.

11. Use stories or examples

People react well to stories or examples, as it makes the content more approachable. Think of this book: haven't the examples made the concepts easier to understand and picture?

My team and I effectively used stories during a communications campaign we did to raise awareness of our employee assistance plan (a benefit scheme where support and/or advice is provided to employees). We had tried numerous times to engage employees with this plan, but nothing seemed to work.

We decided to include stories from fellow employees of how they had used the plan (anonymous of course), doing this to make the plan appear more helpful and approachable to employees. It had a positive result, as participation in the scheme increased.

12. Be genuine

One of the keys to engaging our employees is by building trust, as shown in the 2013 *Forum Global Leadership Pulse* survey. This survey presented data to show a strong correlation between trust and employee engagement. The study found that employees with a low level of trust had an average engagement score of 2.8 (moderate engagement), while those with high trust had an average engagement score of 4.5 (high engagement).

In order to build trust it is key to be genuine. If we sound like a corporate machine, putting no personality into our content, we won't sound genuine and thus will not gain the trust of our employees. Duncan Brown, Head of HR Consultancy at the Institute for Employment Studies, explained it like this:

> However bad or good the news, employees want honesty and clarity. No news is not good news, it's generally interpreted as bad news. They understand that you may not have all the answers but they appreciate being told, ideally face-to face, what you are planning to do with their rewards. So go as early as you can, be straightforward and honest, and tell them 'why' as well as 'what'.

You can sound genuine by:

- **a** Telling the truth – think back to a suggestion previously made about putting yourself in the shoes of your employee. Wouldn't you rather know the truth, even if it is bad news, than not know anything at all?
- **b** Speaking from the heart – there is a quote from Marianne Williamson, a US teacher, author and lecturer that says: 'People hear you on the level you speak to them from. Speak from your heart, and they will hear with theirs.' As she says, if you speak from the heart you will be heard.
- **c** Being believable – when something or someone is believable, it elicits trust, which is exactly what we are trying to achieve by being genuine. One of the key ways of being believable is by being credible. Show your employees through your words that you are competent and credible, and when appropriate, bring in trusted sources to assist you doing this. An example would be having an executive write an introduction to be included in a booklet, giving the booklet credibility. Another example is to have other employees' stories or words included, which makes it more real and believable.

Another impactful quote on the topic of sounding genuine/being honest is something written by Helen Craik, founding Operations Director of Reward Gateway, a leading global employee benefits/engagement technology provider. She said that you should 'be as honest with your people as you can, as early as you can. They'll reward you for it with their understanding and loyalty.' This is a great way to sum up how being genuine is a win for your employees and for your organization.

13. Seek perfection

In the last tip we talked about credibility, and the importance of this when building trust with your employees. One way to remove credibility very quickly is to have errors in your content. What do errors say to your employees: that you didn't care enough to get things right, and/or that you don't know what you are talking about? For this reason you need to double-check all facts, figures, spellings etc, or jeopardize the credibility of your content and ultimately your communications campaign. According to Steve Wartenberg, author (and my brother), you need to 'go over and over what you write until it is perfect, and go over it again a few more times until it really is perfect'.

14. Create breathing room

The concept of 'breathing room' is about creating enough space between your words so that employees have enough space and time to breathe. This is important from an HR communications perspective as we want to give our employees the time to absorb what you have presented to them. You can do this in a few ways:

a Break up your content by using headers, sub-headers etc. This visually shows your employees when they can stop reading a section and take a breath.

b Mix up your context with formatting, fonts etc. This does a few things. It breaks up your content, provides an opportunity for employees to skim the content before reading in depth, or in respect to fonts, mixes things up to make it more visually interesting.

c Use white space with your content. White space is referred to often when talking about design, but it is just as important with words. By having white space, your content appears less daunting, less challenging, as there appear to be fewer words. Think about it: would you read a document where the entire page is covered in text without a break? I find it exhausting, and so will your employees.

15. Test it

It is always a good idea to test your content with someone who can provide an objective opinion. I know that this adds time to the project, and often means that you need to make additional changes, but it is worth the time and effort.

When selecting reviewers to test the content I would suggest selecting a few people. It's helpful to have reviewers with different levels of knowledge on the topic of the communications campaign. For example, using the pensions change example, you may want three people with varying levels of knowledge on pensions to review the content. One person should be a technical expert to ensure that everything is accurate, then maybe a manager level employee with general knowledge, and then another employee who has little to no knowledge of pensions. Now keep in mind this may not always be possible as the information may be extremely confidential. In these instances, you rely on members of your project team, as they will also have varying levels of knowledge.

16. Sleep on it

This is a tip which may seem a bit odd, but was suggested by many of my communication contacts. The suggestion is that you should not rush into finalizing your content. You need to give yourself time to review it one day, maybe another day, and possibly yet another day. What this does is give you multiple perspectives just by looking at it numerous times. This is helpful as you most likely will look at things differently depending on the time of day, your mood etc.

17. Respect legal requirements

I couldn't have a list of HR tips without mentioning legal compliance. As we all know in the HR world, it is critical to respect legal requirements, and include them in content as required. We wouldn't want to put all the effort into developing our content and then find that it is not legally compliant, and thus cannot be used.

A final note about this is that you should consider where and how to include legal language. We need to balance the previous suggestions about keeping our wording simple and engaging with the need to include the legal requirements. You can do this, for example, by having the legal wording in a different section so that it doesn't distract from the more marketing-focused text. Understand where and how it needs to be shown and then review against the other suggestions which have been made.

Now let us turn to **things you should avoid.**

1. Avoid using jargon

The word jargon can be defined as 'words or expressions used by a profession that are difficult for others to understand'. Jargon consists of unfamiliar terms, abstract words, acronyms or abbreviations. I'm sure we've all seen and/or used jargon, and agree that it can be difficult to understand and quite frustrating. I don't know about you, but jargon at times makes me feel like there is a secret club that I haven't been invited to join as I don't get the jargon.

Let's go back to one of the original objectives of effective HR communication which is 'shared meaning'. I ask you: how can we achieve shared meaning if our employees don't understand our content as there is too much jargon? It may be extra work, but challenge yourself to find another word(s) to use, and put the jargon in your desk drawer (meaning put it away).

An example of moving away from jargon is what is commonly being done these days when talking about pensions. It used to be OK to use the word pension when communicating to employees. However, it was found that when employees saw this word they just ignored the content. Many benefit professionals now ban the word pension, instead talking about 'your future', 'your savings' or anything that employees will understand and pay attention to. My challenge to you is: take any HR term and see if you can find a more user-friendly way of explaining it. It can't always be done, but give it a go!

2. Avoid using long and wordy sentences

As the proverb says, 'less is more' – meaning that simplicity and clarity lead to good design. This is definitely true when it comes to writing, as it is critical to express your ideas succinctly. Why? Because we are in an age of directness and making our point more quickly. Also, if you think about it, people will tune out the longer we go on. Some advice is:

- *Stick to one idea per sentence*: it is important to present one idea per sentence to make it more readable. If you have too many ideas you risk confusing your reader.
- *Limit your words*: according to Debi O'Donovan: 'Less is more, try to say it in five instead of ten words, three instead of five words. By doing this you are increasing your ability to have your words read.' Another reason for limiting words is based on the brain's short-term memory and its limited storage capacity. According to a study done by George Miller in 1956 which talks about the 'magical number seven (plus or minus two)', most adults can store between five and nine items in their short-term memory. So if we want our employees

to remember what we are saying, we should limit our words and the length of our sentences.

- *Do not include unnecessary words*: in order to limit your words and fully engage your readers, it is important not to include unnecessary words. Some people call these 'fluff' words, which are words that are light and airy, and have little to no meaning or consequences. This is what we want to avoid, as they distract our employees with empty words.
- *Vary your sentence length*: there is a proverb which says that 'variety is the spice of life'. This means that you need to mix things up, presenting different experiences in order to make life interesting. This is also true when it comes to developing your words and sentences for your communications. Your content will be much more interesting and engaging if you vary your sentence lengths, adding your own 'spice' to your communications.

  An important point to make here is that you want to limit the length of your sentences to no more than 15–20 words. It is fine to vary the sentence length, but keep these guidelines in mind to ensure your communication is effective.

3. Avoid interfering messages

The word interfere means to prevent an action or process from being carried out properly. This is something we want to avoid with our content, as we definitely want our messages to be processed. We can do this by not throwing out too many messages to our employees at one time. Instead, think of ways to break your messages into bite-size pieces. Try to separate your messages into different paragraphs, sections and/or bullets, anything to break then up.

You may have noticed that I've done this with the list of tips. Any time I've found a new message I've created a new point. This was done so that you did not get confused on what the tip was, and so that you did not have information overload. I hope it helped!

4. Avoid negative terms

It can be damaging to use negative words. It may dampen the spirits of your employees, and prevent you from achieving your objectives. Instead, use positive inspiring words that will motivate your employees to an action. An example would be to change 'Do not submit your application after 30 March or you will not be able to join the scheme' to 'Submit your application by 30 March to join the scheme'. It sends the same message, but in a positive manner.

You may have noticed that I've done this in this section. At first I called this section 'things not to do', but changed it to 'things to avoid' as it was less negative and focused on positive actions. I also tried as much as possible to list a tip as a positive and not a negative, ending up with only four tips on what to avoid. However, as you know, sometimes you need to use a negative term or the meaning will be lost. If this is the case, and you cannot change it from a negative to a positive, then try to find a negative which isn't as negative. For example, in this bullet I did not say 'don't ever use negative words', but instead said 'avoid negative terms', which isn't as harsh. Also, consider the emotion that this word will create with your employees. For example, the word 'don't' could make the reader defensive, but the word 'avoid' sounds more like a helpful suggestion.

Through graphics

There is a memorable saying which is that 'a picture is worth a thousand words'. What this means is that a complex idea or thought can often be conveyed effectively using a single image, and can do so better than words. This can be done by using a variety of graphics such as charts, diagrams, tables, images etc, all working in a similar manner to assist us in supporting our words and the overall communications campaign. They do so by engaging and appealing to our employees, capturing their attention and drawing them into the messages.

Another memorable saying is 'seeing is believing', which means that until you see something you won't believe it. This concept of 'belief' is another one of the reasons that graphics are so effective, for many people prefer and/or demand to see a message in addition to reading about it. An example is when I communicated on the topic of a salary sacrifice scheme, so that employees would join the scheme. The way the scheme works is very technical, and thus confusing for employees to understand and accept. This understanding was critical, for if it was not achieved employees would not join and thus benefit from the scheme. For this reason I included diagrams and tables to illustrate the concepts so that employees would both understand and believe the messages being presented. It worked so well that I used the same graphics at my next two companies when developing my communications campaign.

To assist you in developing the most effective content through graphics I have again put together a list of 'what you should do' and 'things to avoid'. You will notice that some of the headers are the same as those used in the previous section about writing. The reason is that often they hold true with graphics as well. Others have been added to address specifically how we can use our graphics to engage and work with our writing to change behaviours and meet our communication objectives.

Here are the ***things you should do***.

1. Think of your employee as a consumer

We need to think of our employees as consumers, 'purchasing' our communication messages. For this reason we need to ensure that our graphics appeal to and engage our employees effectively. Think of how consumer products are marketed and advertised using graphics to appeal to audiences, creating memorable and engaging visuals for them to relate to. Try to find ways where you can similarly use graphics to create this association and meaning. As suggested with words, you should leverage the expertise of your marketing team, asking them to assist you in creating graphics to support your communications campaign.

2. Keep it simple

Keeping it simple holds true not just with words, but with graphics. With words this translates into the way we construct sentences, and with graphics it translates into how we construct the visual images. These images need to be well conceived and carefully executed so that they clearly get across our messages, and do not confuse or distract our employees from these key messages.

For example, if you are including a graph to show how your share price has increased over the years, you wouldn't want to complicate the graph by also showing how your company profits have changed over the years. This would complicate the graph, taking your employees away from the key messages about share price, possibly confusing them at the same time.

3. Support words

It is important that graphics support the key messages of the words we use in our communications campaign. Our graphics should complement our words, and likewise our words should explain the graphics. This means that careful attention needs to be made so that there is a strong relationship between words and text. Neither should sit on their own, meaning that they need to work together to effectively communicate messages.

For example, if you are communicating to employees that the company share scheme is a great way to save and earn money, we wouldn't want to show a graph which shows the share price dropping over the years. Whilst this may be true, it doesn't support your words. In this situation you would need to find another way to gain your employees' trust in the message through graphics. You could possibly create a graphic showing how employees in the past have earned money through the scheme, thus complementing the key message of saving.

4. Think about placement

It is important when integrating graphics into communications material to consider and address their placement. In the previous point I explained how our graphics should support our words, and by placing graphics appropriately they further support and complement our words. Think about it: if I was to explain in writing a concept on one page and the graphics appeared on the next page, would you get the connection? Or, would you be confused by the message on the first page, and further confused by the graphics on the next page? We need to make sure that the communications 'journey' is as easy as possible for our readers, ensuring that all messages are aligned and linked effectively.

Related to the placement of graphics is the size of graphics. For example, if I place a very large graphic next to a short sentence will it overwhelm the message? Will the graphics take over the message? It may or it may not, but my point here is to consider when placing your graphics the size of them in relation to the text and/or other graphics.

5. Use colours strategically

I was introduced to the colour theory by Jim Willis, Managing Director of Bulb Studios (an award-winning digital design agency, specializing in user experience design). According to Jim, by using colours strategically you can help achieve your communication objectives. Did you know that when colours are used correctly they can send a number of messages to your reader or highlight important points? Alternatively, if used incorrectly, colour can quickly confuse your readers and lead them away from your content.

The reason for this is that colours can trigger a variety of emotions and memories. Here are some emotions associated with colours which I've taken from an article written by Hannah Alvarez (2014), who leads the content marketing team at UserTesting:

Red:	Power, passion, love, danger
Orange:	Confidence, cheerfulness, friendliness
Yellow:	Happiness, warmth
Green:	Growth, money, healing, environment, envy
Blue:	Trust, peace, loyalty, masculinity, safety
Purple:	Royalty, mystery, spirituality, creativity
Brown:	Outdoors, food, conservatism, earth
Black:	Formality, luxury, sophistication, death
White:	Purity, simplicity, goodness, freshness

Please keep in mind when referring to this list or any other that you may find/use that colour associations do vary from culture to culture. They also can differ from person to person or even between men and women.

An important practical note about colours is that a significant number of people are colour-blind. Another is to respect your company's branding guidelines. What I mean by this is that, as much as you may want to use a colour to invoke a specific emotion, if your company has guidelines on what colours you can and cannot use, these need to be respected and adhered to first.

6. Get clever and creative

As Debi O'Donovan, founder of the Reward & Employee Benefits Association, explained: 'Little things can make people take notice. Get clever and find ways to get employees talking and take notice through your content.' This is very true when it comes to communication graphics. Effective graphics such as cartoons, photographs, graphs and line drawings can certainly make our employees take notice. And, as Debi says: 'They don't have to be big to make a difference.'

I was inspired to be creative in reading *The Business Playground*, a book by Dave Stewart and Mark Simmons (2010). It talks about linear innovation and linear thinking, explaining that companies doing the same thing over and over again will achieve the same results. The authors encouraged us to make 'creative leaps', exploring the unknown and challenging ourselves to be creative. So my suggestion to you is not to be afraid to take the creative leap to be clever and creative, and to create inspiring and engaging graphics. If I can do it, so can you!

7. Seek perfection

Perfection is critical with graphics as with text, as they support not just employee understanding but employee trust. Have you ever seen a chart or a table in a document which has incorrect data, eg the numbers don't add up? I don't know about you, but when I see this I lose trust in the messages and/or am confused about what is being shared with me. For this reason it is important to double-check all facts, figures etc. A suggestion is to have someone else in your project team be your checker, as often they can catch mistakes that you may have overlooked.

8. Test it

As with words, it is always a good idea to test your graphics. What one image or chart may say to you may present a completely different message to someone else. For this reason, test it with people of different ages, backgrounds etc, to understand their reaction and even their connection to the message. When I think of this point I picture the adverts once used by HSBC Bank. They showed a picture three times, and showed three different meanings for different cultures. This shows how important it is to test meanings before including them in your communications campaign, for as they showed, the message could be completely different.

9. Sleep on it

I'm using this final tip again in respect to graphics, as it is a useful one to keep in mind when planning your communications campaign. In our rush to get things done we may not give ourselves the time to test, and reflect on what we have created. This is especially important in respect to graphics due to the creative nature of them, and thus their ability to invoke different emotions and beliefs. So, as suggested in the section about words, I am again suggesting that you should give yourself time to review your graphics over a period of time.

Finally, here is the one ***thing you should avoid.***

Avoid interfering graphics

I mentioned in the previous section that we do not want our words to interfere with our messages, and the same is true with our graphics. Our graphics should and need to support both our words and our messages. As much as we may like a graphic, if it does not bring these messages 'to life' then we should not include it. I've seen this happen when a talented graphic designer submits something very creative for the communications campaign which unfortunately is so creative that it would not connect with the message. If you and your project team cannot quickly make this connection, then ask your designer to submit different designs, finding one which works.

Things to consider

Thus far in this chapter I've addressed many of the 'normal' or day-to-day things which we need to consider when creating effective communications content. However, I'm sure you would agree that when it comes to communicating with our workforce, things are often far from 'normal'. In this section I am going to address some of these areas, with suggestions on what should be considered when you are in this situation and/or faced with this challenge. The areas I am covering are as follows:

- multi-generational workforces;
- segmentation;
- global audiences;
- branding;
- support material.

Multi-generational workforces

Did you know that we will soon have five generations in the workplace working side by side? In the past we've had three or four generations in the workplace, but never have we had or will we have so many, and thus have to deal with so much diversity. Here are the names of the various generations for your reference. Please note that depending on the source, different dates are given, so keep this in mind:

- Silent Generation – born before 1942.
- Baby Boomers – born following World War II, from early 1940s up to early 1960s.
- Generation X – born early/mid-1960s to early 1980s.
- Generation Y – born early/mid-1980s to early 2000s.
- Generation Z – born mid-2000s.

This creates challenges for us in HR, not only in the design of our HR programmes, but in how we communicate these programmes and other key HR messages. So why are there generational differences and thus communication challenges? There has been a lot written on this topic, and various theories and points of view. To keep things simple, I've broken these differences down into two main categories: upbringing and stage of life.

Upbringing

This refers to what someone has been exposed to and/or experienced as they were growing up. This influences how they like and expect to be communicated to, as this is their 'sphere of reference', meaning it is what they have been exposed to as they have been growing up.

To illustrate this, let me share with you a rough timeline on when the various communication technologies were first used. I've started with the first communications 'technology', just to make a point that we've been communicating for quite a long time.

FIGURE 5.2 Technology timeline

Roman Times	1970s	1980s	1990s	2000	2010+
Fire	Work computers	Home computers	Mobile phones Company intranet Text messaging	Social media Smartphones	Tablets

As you can see from Figure 5.2, based on when someone was born and when they began working, they would have had exposure to some or all of these communication technologies. This not only impacts which medium they are comfortable with, but also how content is best presented to them. For example, if you are accustomed to receiving messages without technology or through basic technology (eg e-mails), you may be more comfortable with more lengthy and/or detailed content. You may also be more comfortable with face-to-face communication, for again, this is what is/was 'normal' to you. If on the other hand you have grown up with newer technologies that focus on more high-level or succinct communication, you would prefer more 'sound bytes', meaning more concise communication content. The generations in the middle, eg Baby Boomers and possibly Gen X, fall somewhere in the middle, as they want some details and some 'sound bytes', but are somewhere in between the other generations.

Stage of life

This refers to where someone is in their life, and thus what is important and really matters to them. This influences their beliefs and behaviours, and in respect to communications it impacts what will create a 'call to action' for them.

To illustrate this, Table 5.2 lists some of the major life events and/or challenges which we face during our working lives which impact what stage of life we are in.

Depending on which of these events you are dealing with, you will react differently to the communication content. For example, if I was reaching my retirement, I would want content which focused on what I needed to do as I got to this milestone. If I was 10 years from retirement I may be more interested in what I needed to do to ensure my pension pot was big enough to support my impending retirement. Finally, if I was many years away from retirement, the communication content may need to focus on why it is

TABLE 5.2 Major life events

• Student debt	• Eldercare costs
• House purchase	• Dual incomes
• Birth of a child	• Promotions
• Childcare cost	• Retirement

important to start a pension scheme now and not wait. Different stage of life, different communication content.

A point I'd like to make that relates to both of these categories is that it is critical to put yourself in the shoes of each generation. Think about what each generation wants and needs to receive from you in respect to content. In order for it to be meaningful and actionable it needs to 'speak' to them using words and graphics which reflect their upbringing and stage of life. Put yourself in their shoes, considering what they as a Gen X, Gen Y, new parent, new manager etc want and need to hear and see. If you don't know what this is, then as I've said before, go out and talk to your employees who are in these generations and/or situations. Find out what works for them, and create your content accordingly.

My final point to make in this section about multi-generations is that you don't want to make the mistake of generalizations and stereotypes. Just because you have employees in specific generations and/or at different stages of life does not mean that they all have the same needs or behaviours of the generation. We all bring different experiences to work, and are in different situations. This is based on what I've said earlier, which is upbringing and stage of life, but it could also be influenced by your personality, your previous experiences, your family etc. For example, I'm in a generation where the books say that as I didn't grow up with technology I like to receive detailed information and don't necessarily like it done through the newer technologies such as social media and texts. Yes, I do like details to support the content, but I would much prefer the 'sound bytes' which are being asked for by the younger generations. This is because of my personality, which is one which moves and acts quickly, which (anyone who has worked with me knows) means that I like to get to the point quickly. The trick here is to create content which addresses the needs of all of the generations in one way, and provide this to everyone. This may not always be possible, as we will discuss in the section about segmentation, but it is a good starting point for your content.

Segmentation

In the last section I addressed the challenge of communicating to a diverse workforce, ending the section saying that sometimes the best way to handle these challenges is through segmentation. This is something which is being discussed and is used more frequently in the HR world thanks to our colleagues in marketing. Marketers have been using segmentation as a way to communicate to their customers, which has resulted in customers who are more loyal, and ultimately spend more with them. An example is what some of the big online retailers do, using their customers' purchasing history to make recommendations on what they may want to buy in the future, tempting them to spend more. Another example is what other retailers do when they again use their customers' purchasing history to send them discount vouchers on products they've bought in the past. This again tempts customers to come in and make more purchases. These are both examples of using data on customers to understand what will suit their audiences, what they will react to, and how they will be influenced. No wonder we in HR are interested in using this technique!

So what is segmentation and how can we use it in HR communications? It can be defined as a process where you subdivide a large group into 'clearly identifiable segments having similar needs, wants or demand characteristics'. From an HR communications perspective it can be a way to divide our employees into communication groups so that the content is targeted to motivate and engage them in the most effective manner. According to Capita's 2014 *Employee Insight Report*, different employees want different things at different times in their working lives, and by segmenting your audience, you are addressing these differences.

As discussed in the last section, it may be based on the generation of the employee, but it may also be based on differences in job levels, salaries, geography etc. An example would be segmenting your employees for your annual flexible benefits communication campaign. (*Note*: A flexible benefits scheme is when employees are given a choice/list of benefits which they select based on their individual needs.) According to the Towers Watson 2014 *Flexible Benefits Research*, 41 per cent of companies responding send targeted messages to their employees about the flexible benefits scheme, and a further 25 per cent are considering doing so. These companies segment their employees based on their age, gender, job level and/or benefits they currently have in place, sending them different targeted messages. What this does is help promote and educate employees on the benefits which are likely to be of most interest and relevance to them personally. The result is that companies have more employees selecting benefits as they understand the WIIFM (what's in it for me). Had they not received this clear message, they may not have taken the actions which would have best suited their needs.

Another example of segmentation may be segmenting employees based on the role they play in an HR programme. For example, if you are communicating on a performance appraisal process you may want to segment the communication to managers (who have one role to play) and another to non-managerial employees (who have a different role to play). This focuses the communications content on exactly what they need to know and do, to ensure they meet the needs of their role. If the communication is generic, then managers/employees may miss critical information and steps to follow.

Technology has enabled segmentation, making it easier to first break out the groups, and second to manage the separate communications. By creating rules through technology it can be fairly straightforward to manage this previously complex task. However, I do want to point out that although much can be automated, we in HR still need to develop the segmented communications content and our IT colleagues will need to create and manage segmentation codes. For this reason I would suggest that you question and challenge each segment, ensuring that there truly is a reason for them to be different. If you cannot clearly explain the need for separate groups, meaning that they have the same communication needs and actions, then do not create separate groups. Even if you find, for example, that you have four generations in your workforce, don't automatically segregate the communications; ask yourself if it is needed.

An example of how a company has used segmentation in a communications campaign is what LV= did with their pensions communication campaign (see case study on p 177 for more details). They segmented their employees into two groups: those who were directly being impacted by the pension change, and those that were not, but still needed to know what was going on in the business. They created different communication material and different content for each group. By doing this LV= was creating relevance for the two very diverse audiences. Had they not done this, both groups may not have responded as well as they did to the material and content, achieving the success they did in their communications campaign.

Global audiences

We live and work in a world where there is an increasing amount of globalization. As businesses expand globally it connects us in many ways, but it also highlights our differences. What this means from a communications perspective is that we need to balance global messaging with respecting local differences. There is a term which is used often when we create our HR programmes, which is 'glocal'. 'Glocal' can be defined as making global and local considerations, and is exactly what we need to do when developing our communications content.

Here are some suggestions to assist in developing content for global audiences.

1. Keep it simple

As discussed earlier in the chapter, it is important to keep content simple. It is even more important when developing content for global audiences for a few reasons. The first reason is because it will be easier to have it translated (which will save you time and/or money). The second reason is that, when translated, it will be easier for your audience to understand.

2. Use graphics

Graphics are helpful in getting a point and/or a message across easily and quickly. For this reason, graphics are extremely useful when communicating to global audiences. What may take many words to communicate, could be done in a simple and clear graphic.

It is important to consider differences in meaning when using graphics. Keep in mind the global bank example again, where the same picture shown to people in different countries had different meanings. The one I liked the best was a picture of high-heeled shoes, where one global audience used the word 'pleasure' to describe the picture and another used the word 'pain' to describe the same picture. So true for both!

3. Consider differences in terminology

There are times when a word can mean one thing in one country and something completely different in another country. I learned this first hand, and the hard way, when I moved from the United States to the United Kingdom to live and work. Although both countries use the English language, I was amazed at how many words had different meanings. I'm too embarrassed to share with you my mistakes, but trust me, I made them!

My first suggestion would be to consider differences which you already know when developing your content. For example, if you know that one word may have a different and/or negative meaning in another country, try to find another word to use. The second suggestion would be to ask global business partners to review your content. Ask them to point out if there are any words or graphics which may be confusing and/or convey the wrong message.

4. Avoid colloquial words/terms

The word 'colloquial' means that it is used in ordinary or familiar conversation, and could be considered informal or casual. A few examples are 'ain't', which means that you are not going to do something, and 'gonna', which means going to do. These words/terms should be avoided when developing content for global audiences as they may be difficult to understand and/or confusing.

My suggestion would be to find another way of saying this word/term. It may mean adding a few words, but it will assist in your audience understanding the message.

5. Avoid country/cultural specifics

There are some words that are specific to one country or culture. An example is the NHS, which in the UK is the National Health Service, or NI, which in the UK is National Insurance. Whilst this has a meaning in the UK, it will not translate when you are communicating to employees in other countries. In these situations it would be better to use a generic term such as 'health service' or 'local taxes'.

Branding

The last topic I'm going to address in this chapter is branding, as it is something to consider when developing your communications content and your communications campaign. The definition of a brand is a name, term, design, symbol etc that distinguishes one product from another. Brands are used by businesses to differentiate themselves from one another, and in HR to create an association or connection with a programme and/or a message. By having an effective brand, it will create something recognizable for your employees, which can influence their behaviours and actions.

Here are some suggestions to assist in developing a brand for your communications campaign.

1. Decide if you want/need a brand

The first suggestion is the starting point, which is whether or not you need a brand for your communications campaign. There may be some situations when a brand will be useful, and there are other situations where a brand may not be necessary. There are no set rules on this, but ask yourself if by having a brand for your campaign it will make a difference. If it will, then create a brand, but if it is not needed/necessary, then do not create a brand. An example would be if you were communicating a one-time HR change such as changing working hours. Do you need something recognizable in this situation? Not really. If, however, you are communicating a new flexible way of working, you may want to create a brand. By having a brand, you will enable employees to understand and relate to the messages now and in the future about flexible working.

Think about whether your communication on this topic will have a life, meaning that over time there will be multiple messages. If it doesn't, you don't need a brand. If it will, you may, but you don't automatically need one; only if it is something which you need to be recognizable.

2. Link to the messages

As mentioned earlier in this chapter, you want your content to stick together; thus the brand will need to link to the key messages. For example, if your communications campaign is about saving for your retirement, create a brand which stands for this. I've seen piggy-banks used in these situations, which is a great way of visually linking to the message of saving for your future. Whatever you design, make sure that it complements and links to the messages, and doesn't distract and/or confuse the messages.

3. Keep it simple

The word 'simplicity' has occurred many times throughout this chapter, and that is because I strongly believe that simplicity is key in communications. When it comes to the brand, it needs to be simple enough to be easily recognizable and associated with the content and key messages. If it is not understood quickly then it is not fulfilling its objectives. This is especially important when communicating to multiple generations and/or global audiences, as the connection can be even more challenging.

Conclusion

This chapter has been both a pleasure and a challenge to write. The reason is that I believe in and have seen the impact that effective communications content can have on a communications campaign. If we can get it right, we can create the 'stickiness' that I mentioned at the beginning of the chapter. This is important, as it will make our employees want to focus on the content and visit it time and time again. It is also important because it will move your employees to the desired changed behaviours and/or calls to action. There is, however, a lot to consider; thus we have the challenges which we face as we create our content (eg multi-generational workforces, global workforces etc). But if we focus on the guiding principles of creating content which is valuable, relevant and consistent, we have a much better chance of getting it right, meeting our communications campaign objectives and positively impacting our business. Put your writer hat on again, and think of what you can do through both your words and your graphics so that your 'book' will be a best-seller which your employees will 'buy'.

Top tips on content

- Create content which will make your messages stick, creating the 'stickiness' that will make your employees read it over and over again.
- Create content which will encourage your employees to read, think and behave differently.
- Follow the guiding principles of content, which are to create valuable, relevant and consistent content.
- Create words and graphics which are simple to understand and associate with, and link to your key messages.
- Determine if/when segmentation would be helpful in ensuring that your content is appropriate to your different employee groups.
- Consider the multi-generational workforce when creating content: what is their 'sphere of influence' which they will refer to when taking in communications content?
- Consider how your content will work with global audiences, and whether you need to adapt to ensure it is effective globally.

Skills for being an effective writer

- Ability to weave together and create a compelling 'story' which will capture and engage your audience through effective content.
- Ability to develop creative and appealing graphics to support your key messages.
- Ability to be a simplifier – being able to take complex concepts and/or messages and present in a meaningful and straightforward manner.
- Ability to develop effective content to deal with a variety of situations and/or challenges.
- Strong attention to detail, with ability to identify and resolve errors.
- Ability to understand differences in audiences based on age, gender, culture etc.
- Being a perfectionist, not being satisfied until everything is 100 per cent perfect.

References

Alvarez, H (2014) *A Guide to Color, UX and Conversion Rates*, https://www.usertesting.com/blog/2014/12/02/color-ux-conversion-rates/ [accessed 2 October 2015]

Capita (2014) Employee Insight Report 2014, https://www.capitaemployeebenefits.co.uk/en/Current-News/2014/05/Employee-Insight-Report-2014.aspx [accessed 2 October 2015]

Doctorow, EL [nd] http://www.brainyquote.com/quotes/authors/e/e_l_doctorow.html

The Forum Corporation (2013) *Driving Business Results by Building Trust: Findings from 2013 Global Forum Global Leadership Pulse Survey*, http://www.forum.com/ [accessed 2 October 2015]

Harvard Business School [2001] What makes a good leader, *Harvard Business School Alumni*, https://www.alumni.hbs.edu/stories/Pages/story-bulletin.aspx?num=3059 [accessed 2 October 2015]

HSBC (2007) http://culturemaking.typepad.com/.shared/image.html?/photos/uncategorized/2007/11/16/hsbc3.png [accessed 2 October 2015]

Miller, GA (1956) The magical number seven, plus or minus two: Some limits on our capacity for processing information, *The Psychological Review*, **63**, 81–97

Rand, A (2007) *Atlas Shrugged*, Penguin Books, London

Stewart, D and Simmons, M (2010) *The Business Playground: Where creativity and commerce collide*, Pearson Education, Harlow, Essex

Towers Watson (2014) Flexible Benefits Research, http://www.employeebenefits.co.uk/benefits/flexible-benefits/employee-benefits-/-towers-watson-flexible-benefits-research-2014/104459.article [accessed 2 October 2015]

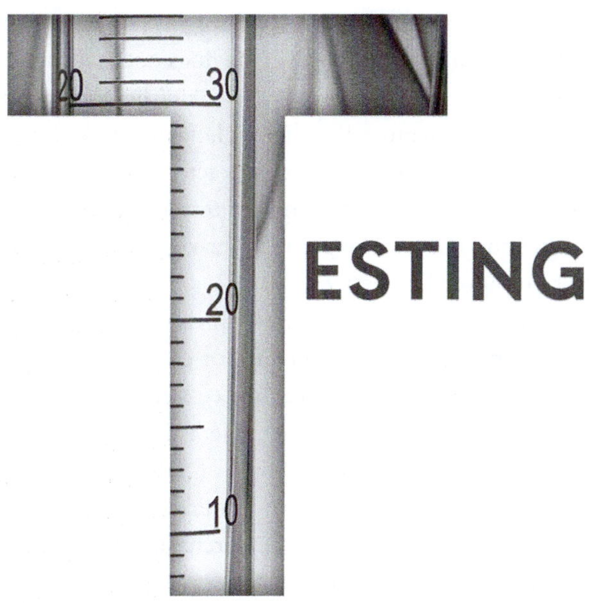

TESTING

Testing

06

Introduction

In this final chapter we will explore the process of testing, both why it is important and what you can do to test effectively. A good way to begin thinking of this concept is to think of a pilot flying an aeroplane. After the pilot logs the flight plan and takes off he/she does not just sit there and have a cup of tea or coffee, hoping for the best. He/she continually monitors where the aeroplane is against the flight plan and makes adjustments as required to ensure it is on course. This is exactly what we need to do with our communications campaign: continually test and monitor it to ensure it is 'on track', adjusting it if it is not going in the right direction so that we can deliver against our agreed objectives.

I'd like you to wear the hat of a *tester* in this chapter. Testers, whether they are testing computer apps or software or conducting market research, are the people that follow a structured process to continually review and interpret how well things are going in a project. They ask the question, 'Are we achieving the predicted results?' Think of a tester of a new computer app, testing the app over and over again to make sure that it works on any computer or mobile device and for anyone purchasing it. Or think of a market researcher, testing a sample group of customers to see if their new product is something which they will buy. Our employees are 'purchasing' our communication messages, so it is just as critical to ensure that it is working for them. And just like apps or products, which need adjustments and refinements even after they are brought to market, so do our communication campaigns, again ensuring that they are on course. It is important that we continually review our employees' feedback and reactions, adjusting what or how we are communicating as required.

In this chapter we will cover the following:

- Why should we test?
- What to test.
- When to test.

- Methods for testing.
- How to test.

Why should we test?

Before I answer this question of why we should test, we should consider Thomas Edison, a famous US inventor who lived in the 19th century. Edison was the inventor of the light bulb, the phonograph and the motion picture camera, to name just a few. These were all brilliant creations which have had a huge influence on our everyday lives. However, not everything Mr Edison created was a success; he also had quite a few failures. But as he was quoted saying: 'I have not failed 10,000 times, I've successfully found 10,000 ways that will not work'. He also said: 'I am not discouraged, because every wrong attempt discarded is another step forward'. These quotes show the power of trial and error, helping to bring us closer to our 'inventions' and achieving our objectives. We, like Edison, are going to make mistakes and/or encounter challenges throughout our communications campaign. It is what we do to uncover these through testing and resolve through implementation which will make our communications campaign a success or a failure.

Here are some other reasons why we should test.

Gives us a starting point

Testing gives us a starting point, a way to gauge how well the communications campaign will do in the future. Sometimes this involves testing, whether it be formal or informal, and other times it just involves pulling data. For example, if the objective of our campaign is to increase participation in a benefits scheme, our starting point would be to find out how many employees we currently have in the scheme. If, however, the aim of the campaign is to increase understanding and appreciation of this same benefit scheme, we would need to test employees to find out how well they understand and appreciate the scheme before we launch the campaign. By doing this we will be able to determine if we've achieved our objectives. If we don't do this, how will we know?

It identifies if we are on track

During the investigation phase we talked about how our objectives help us define success. One of the key reasons for testing is to see how on track we are at achieving these objectives. Using the situation explained above in which we want to know if our communications campaign has caused employees to have a better understanding of the new benefit scheme, by conducting an informal test in the middle of the communications campaign we can identify if our campaign is working and on track. If we are on track, great, we continue with our campaign; if we are not, we use the feedback to determine how best to make changes. The benefit of this is that we have time to change the campaign before it is too late, and the campaign has finished with us not achieving our objectives.

It identifies changes required

Once we identify that we are not on track, testing is the best way to help us identify how to handle this, and what changes need to be made. Let's continue with our example where we identify that our communications campaign is not achieving our objective of increasing understanding and appreciation of our benefits scheme. We may be surprised with this, as our employees told us during the investigation phase that they wanted a booklet to explain the scheme to them. But what we hear during the testing phase is that, although the booklet was great, it was more than they had expected and didn't answer all of their questions. With this we could possibly create a one-page summary, add FAQs (frequently asked questions) and/or conduct education sessions based on our conversations with employees. Testing helps us come up with these solutions. Going back to Edison, they help us use our mistakes from our previous inventions to come up with an amazing invention.

Allows you to celebrate successes

Another benefit of testing is that it allows you to celebrate your successes when they occur, both during and at the end of your campaign. If you don't test, how will you know your achievements and thus be able to celebrate your successes? Testing brings it all together, helping you review and analyse your results against your objectives and celebrate the success of achieving them (which I'm sure you will!).

Proves ROI and effectiveness

Last but not least, one of the key reasons to test is to be able to provide hard data to prove to the business the ROI (return on investment) of your communications campaign, and the effectiveness to the business. Think back to Mr Edison and his invention of the light bulb. What would have happened if no one ever bought the light bulb; would it still have been considered a success? Probably not, for although it was an innovative invention, businesses are driven by results. For this reason we need to be able to show these positive results to prove our worth and effectiveness. By showing hard outcomes and hard business KPIs (key performance indicators) our communications campaign (and future campaigns) will be taken seriously and given the business respect and support that we require.

What to test

When deciding what to test it is important to go right back to your objectives. Remind yourself of what you are trying to achieve as a result of your communications campaign, and decide what test data will help you assess if you are achieving this. This set of objectives becomes your test measures or your KPIs. It is important to begin your campaign with this clear set of objectives, as this will ensure you have the necessary focus and will help you end up with a more effective testing tool.

The next point to make regarding test data is that there are two types of data that can be tested: primary and secondary data. Primary data is what we most often think about when we think about test data, and can be described as fresh or new data. Secondary data is a type of data which is often ignored and/or forgotten, and can be described as data which has been gathered in the past. For example, previous surveys which you or someone else in HR and/or the business have conducted. This type of data should be paid attention to, for if not we are missing a trick by not using this already accessible data. Besides having some or all of what we need, secondary data can potentially save you time and money. Andy Brown, CEO of Engage, shared with me the analogy of looking in the cupboard before going out shopping when explaining the power of secondary data. I think this analogy is a great way of thinking about it: I don't know about you, but I've gone to the shop many times only to come home and find that I had the product tucked away in my cupboard already. A suggestion would be to look first at what you have through secondary data, and then determine what primary data needs to be collected to supplement this.

The data you collect from both primary and secondary tests can be categorized as either qualitative or quantitative data. I've highlighted in Figure 6.1 the key differences between these categories.

Whether you select quantitative or qualitative measures depends on your objectives and test measure KPIs. Often it works best to use a bit of both and/or switch from one category to another. As explained in a previous example in this chapter, if your objective is to increase participation in a

FIGURE 6.1 Qualitative and quantitative measures

Quantitative

- Expressed in numerical terms such as numbers or ratios.
- Allows you to answer 'what', 'how many' and 'when' questions.
- Examples include enrolment or participation numbers, engagement scores, turnover statistics.

Qualitative

- Expressed descriptively.
- Allows you to address questions about 'why' and 'how', as well as pulling perceptions, attitudes and beliefs.
- Examples include employee awareness, understanding or behavioural changes.

benefits scheme, you would want to test how participation rates change, which is a qualitative measure. If during testing, however, you find that employees are not joining the scheme, you may need to collect descriptions from employees to answer the question 'why' (eg why are they not enrolling in the benefits scheme), which is qualitative information. By switching to this measure you can get a full picture of the situation, which can help you make decisions as to how to alter the communications campaign so that understandings and/or perceptions can change.

Once you decide which test category(s) you will use, the next step is to decide exactly what you want/need to test. I've listed below some general guidelines to help you decide what to test for your communications campaign. Keep these points in mind and/or refer to them as you select and create your test measures:

Collect useful information

Ask yourself, what am I going to do with this information? Is it going to improve my understanding of the campaign, help me make decisions etc? Is it something that I need to know, or something that would be nice to know? If it has no real purpose, then don't include it.

For example, don't ask a qualitative question such as 'Are you happy with the messaging?' if your campaign is delivering a negative change to employees (eg reducing holiday entitlement). Why are you asking this, what are you going to do with it? Of course the employees will say that they are not happy with the messaging, as it is a negative message. You don't need this information. A better question to ask is 'Do you understand the reason for the change?' This will help you understand if the message is getting through and/or if you need to make any changes in your communication campaign.

Collect timely information

Just as important as useful information is timely information. What I mean by this is that you should only ask questions/collect information that you will have the opportunity to action as part of the communications campaign.

A great example of this occurred during LV='s pension change communications campaign (see the case study on p 177). As part of their campaign they allowed employees to submit questions on the pension change. These questions, along with the answers, were then posted on the intranet site created as part of this communication campaign. Originally the project team sanitized the questions before posting, meaning they cleaned them up a bit, as they felt it would make them easier for employees to understand. However, they received feedback from employees saying that they didn't want their questions changed as it felt as if the company was doing this to control the questions and answers. As a key objective of the campaign was to gain the trust of employees, LV= quickly changed their strategy and posted questions exactly as they were submitted. By reacting to employee feedback in a timely manner they were able to turn what could have been a negative factor of their campaign into a more powerful positive factor. Had they not asked the question during the testing, this result would not have been achieved.

Evaluate in a constructive manner

What I mean by this statement is that all information obtained during testing should be considered, whether it is positive or negative. Yes it would be great to receive only positive quantitative and qualitative information, but that isn't reality, and we need to be prepared to react to both positive and negative. Keep in mind that it is helpful and constructive to the success of your communications campaign to have both.

Think of the LV= example where they quickly reacted to the negative feedback by updating their communications campaign. What would have happened if they had ignored the slightly negative feedback from employees and not changed their strategy on how to deal with questions? They most likely would not have achieved their campaign objectives. As you will see in the case study, LV= far exceeded their objectives by not only creating an amazing communications campaign, but by having a flexible approach to reacting to their testing information, both positive and negative.

Track and assess what has changed

It is important to track and assess what has changed, both intended and unintended. Intended changes are those that you are trying to achieve as part of your communications campaign, and are normally part of your testing plan. For example, if you are measuring how many employees enrol in the new benefits scheme, you would be tracking the intended change in the number of new enrolees.

It is just as important to measure unintended change so that you can understand and interpret the reasons for the change. Using the example of a new benefits scheme, you may find that as a result of the campaign there is an increased number of employees joining another benefit scheme. You need to understand why this is happening and possibly if it is desirable. Are employees confused by the new scheme, which is making them join something which they don't need to join? Is this desirable or is this something which could have a negative impact on them? It is important to assess this unintended change and determine if/how it impacts the overall communications campaign.

Think of testing from all angles

When it comes to testing, it is important to test from a multitude of angles. For example, yes, you can obtain helpful information from your employees, but can you also obtain helpful information from others such as your management team, union representatives etc? By testing from different angles and being able to look through a multitude of 'lenses' you are able to look at and measure data from different perspectives.

Another thing that LV= did brilliantly as part of their pensions communications campaign was to measure the success of their campaign directly through business partners. They held weekly calls with business partners in the various functions and office locations to discuss how the campaign was going. This provided an opportunity to receive important qualitative information from these colleagues, looking at feedback from a different and useful angle.

When to test

It is important to decide up-front how often and when you are going to conduct your tests. I would suggest that you test multiple times throughout your communications campaign, as it will give you a better indication if you are 'on track'. However, that doesn't mean that you should test for the sake of testing, but using the guidelines I listed in the first section, test when you feel you will receive information that is useful and timely. Here are some general guidelines on when and why to test at the following key times during your communications campaign.

Before the campaign

It can be helpful to conduct a test before the communications campaign for a few reasons. The first reason is that it can provide you with information to help you develop your communications campaign. An example of this was when BT conducted a test prior to their communications campaign. Their campaign involved communicating to employees who had company shares maturing through their 'saveshare' plan (see the case study on p 171). BT conducted an online survey with their employees before the campaign began, asking them what information they needed in order to make the right choices and take the appropriate actions. The data collected shaped their communications campaign as it pointed out to the BT team that one of the most important pieces of information requested was information on tax consequences. Had they not surveyed employees they would have included information as a matter of course, but probably not at the level requested by employees.

The second reason to test before the campaign begins is to give you a starting point. This starting point gives you a baseline of data which you can track against throughout the campaign. Using the BT example, one of the objectives of their campaign was to inform/educate those employees who had shares maturing through the 'saveshare' plan, but also to raise awareness on the plan to the general population. Their starting point/baseline was the percentage of employees who were in the plan, which they could test again at the end of the campaign.

During the campaign

It can also be helpful to conduct a test(s) throughout the communications campaign for a few reasons. The first reason is to ensure that you are on track against your objectives – one of the reasons for testing. If you are not, then you still have time to adjust your campaign before it ends – another reason for testing. An example would be if you were conducting a communications campaign to increase participation in an HR programme. From your starting point/baseline number you can test, either formally or informally, during the campaign to see how this number is changing and how the campaign is progressing. If the number is not changing then you can further test to understand why, and adjust accordingly.

The second reason is related to the first in that it prevents surprises. I don't know about you, but I don't like surprises, or as we call them in the United States 'curve balls' (they're called curve balls as the ball is not thrown straight and thus the hitter cannot hit it). If you test during the campaign you can keep an eye on the 'ball' or data, and do something so that the 'hitter' can connect with the ball, or in the HR world, the employee can connect with the message.

At the end of the campaign

Testing at the end of the campaign is often the most common time to test for the reasons stated at the start of this chapter, which are to celebrate successes, prove your ROI and prove the effectiveness of your communications campaign. Using the BT example, one of their objectives was to increase participation in their 'saveshare' plan, and by testing at the end of the campaign they were able to prove that they did just this. As shown in the full case study, they were extremely successful in their communications campaign, increasing participation in their UK plan by 7 per cent and their international plan by 9 per cent. Had they not tested at the end they would not have had visibility to these achievements.

The final point to make about when to test is that only you can make this decision. Put your tester hat on, and think about when and how often you need to test in order to collect the data which you require.

Methods for testing

There are a variety of mechanisms/methodologies for testing, which depend again on your objectives and KPIs. They also depend on whether you require quantitative or qualitative information. I've provided below examples of some of the most common methodologies.

Formal surveys

Formal surveys are used to collect quantitative data from a group or sample of respondents. They can be paper-based or done online, and are helpful when you need to collect data from a large number of people and/or target a specific group. They are also helpful when you want to compare data between groups quite easily. They can be done quite simply using a variety of techniques or mechanisms, and questions can be structured to include answers using rating scales (eg 1 to 5) or short answers (yes or no).

Formal surveys can provide useful and reliable data, having high response rates and quality data, but only if they are constructed and delivered well. Below are some tips on how to create effective surveys:

- *Keep the survey short*: Think about it: would you want to participate in a survey that takes a long time to complete? The same is true with your employees, as you will get more respondents if you create shorter, more focused surveys. Make sure that each question you ask addresses your original objectives and KPIs, and is not just 'nice to know'. Keep this focus and you will ensure that your survey is short and to the point, and you will get higher rates of participation.
- *Keep questions short*: As with the survey, you want your questions to be short and focused. If a question goes on too long and/or is confusing, your employees will not answer it, or will answer it incorrectly as they do not understand what is being asked. Try to make your survey questions as specific and direct as possible, challenging yourself to get to the point as quickly and effectively as possible. By doing this you will obtain better quality data from your respondents.
- *Be consistent*: Whether you decide to use a rating scale or short answers, it is important to be consistent throughout your survey. For example, if you have a rating scale of 1 to 5 at the start of your survey and then change to a rating scale of 1 to 3 later in your survey, it will confuse and/or frustrate your employees. Select something which will work throughout the survey, and stick with it.
- *Be logical*: Nothing frustrates me more than a survey which jumps all over the place, not having a flow or logic. If it frustrates me it will certainly frustrate your employees, which reduces your chances of them responding and/or responding correctly. For this reason it is important to map out your questions and put them in a logical order, one which will not only make sense, but be easy for your employees to follow and complete.

Focus groups

Focus groups are used to obtain qualitative data by conducting group interviews with a relatively small number of participants, generally between 5 and 12 people. Participants are asked questions or are given statements to which they share their thoughts, opinions or reactions. These are helpful in that you can quickly obtain data directly from your employees, can observe their reactions, and can also follow up with additional questions as required. Below are some tips on how to conduct effective focus groups:

- *Have a good moderator*: It is important to have a good moderator leading the focus groups, as they can make the difference between a good or a bad session. Qualities of a good moderator are someone who has strong people skills to include being able to listen and encourage participation. They should also be able to frame questions well and manage questions and challenges as they arise. Finally, they should be able to remain neutral during the discussion, thus not influencing the direction or outcome of the conversation.
- *Keep focus*: As they are called 'focus' groups, it should be no surprise that I'm suggesting that they need to have focus. There are two ways to maintain focus. The first is to make sure that the questions and topics you are raising are specific enough and linked back to your objectives. You have a short amount of time, so focus on what is really important. The second way to maintain focus is to keep the conversation on track, sticking to the questions and topics you have created for these sessions. This can be difficult as participants may try to change the direction or raise additional questions, but if you want to collect the data you need as part of this test, then the moderator needs to keep this focus or risk not achieving the test objectives.
- *Consider the setting*: The setting of the focus group can make a big difference in your ability to collect data. The environment needs to be non-threatening so that participants feel comfortable being open and honest when responding to questions and providing input. In order to do this you should think of the physical environment (eg appropriate seating, confidential space) as well as the mix of participants. When inviting and selecting participants you should think of how they will mix together in a focus group. For example, by mixing managers and subordinates will you be able to maintain an open and honest setting? Also, think about how you will need to break down data (eg by job level, age etc), and consider this when constructing your groups.
- *Keep sessions short*: As with other testing mechanisms, you want to keep your focus group sessions as short as possible. The first reason for doing this is to respect your participants' time, which is important in gaining their trust and cooperation. The second reason is that you don't want to cover too much in a session, or you risk losing the

interest and engagement of your participants. Think about it: how long can you sit still without starting to stare into space and think of other things? Keep this in mind and focus your sessions on what is important and what can reasonably be covered.

To end this section on focus groups I want to point out a slightly different type of focus group, which is called an 'employee lab'. These are bigger events where you invite 40–50 participants at a time as opposed to 5–12 for a focus group. These are helpful if you need to focus on a bigger and/or strategic topic or question. The way they work is that you break the larger group into smaller groups, asking them to discuss and debate the topic, and report back on their thoughts and solutions. According to Andy Brown, CEO of Engage, they are extremely helpful as they tend to create a more collaborative discussion as the groups are given the opportunity to challenge, explore and look at root causes before reporting back to the larger group.

Social engagement apps

Social engagement apps are another mechanism for obtaining useful and reliable data from your employees. Over the years they have become a more common and expected way of communicating in both our personal and professional lives. Retailers and marketers use them frequently as a way to invite customers/consumers into a social relationship with their brand, and to collect consumer information. They have become very clever at finding ways to make them engaging, simple and even motivational as many offer chances to win prizes by participating.

In HR we are also using these techniques, using apps to engage with our 'consumers' or employees, as well as to collect our test data. They work well for us as part of our communications campaign as they are very agile and user-friendly, and help us gather data faster, in more real time. For example, you can go out to employees through the app at the start of the communications campaign to ask questions, and then if in the middle of the campaign you find you have other questions, you can quickly send them out through the app. Below are some tips on how to create effective social engagement apps:

- *Keep it clean and simple*: As with the other testing methods, it is important to keep the number of questions you ask short as well as the length of the questions themselves. Keep your test short and simple, focusing on the specific data you require, making it fast and easy to use. The first reason for this is that, if the testing elements are too long, then your users will not take the time to participate. Another reason is that as apps are often used on mobile devices or smaller screens, readers will find it difficult to have too much on the screen. The final reason is related to how people use apps, meaning that often they use them as they walk down the street, waiting in a queue etc. For this reason you need to keep things short, as their attention span is shorter in these physical situations.

- *Personalize the experience*: One of the great things about apps is that they are relatively easy to personalize. This means that you can personalize the questions being sent to different groups of employees, and thus personalize their experience. For example, if you have one group of employees that have not engaged with your new HR programme, you can send them questions to understand why they have not done so and/or remind them to take this action. This is helpful in that it doesn't push information to those that don't need it, which means that they will take notice if/when you do go to them in the future. Also, as humans we take more notice when something is more personal to us, and thus does not seem to be a generic message.
- *Motivate users to come back*: As I mentioned at the start of this section, social engagement apps are a great way to keep going back to your employees for additional information. In order to do this you need to create an experience which is compelling enough so that they will come back and/or motivate and/or entice them to come back another way. One way to do this is what retailers do, which is to offer a prize, which can be a relatively inexpensive way to create excitement and engagement. I've offered prizes as small as a £5 gift certificate, which although it may not sound like a lot, my employees were excited about as they love to win something. Another way which is not financial is by making the app itself interesting and/or exciting to use, which thus engages your employees. Using tips from retailers, you want to make the app eye-catching, uncluttered and intuitive.

How to test

Once you select what you want to test and the method you will use to get the best data, the next thing to consider is how you are going to conduct your test. Though they may vary, depending on the method you select, there are seven basic steps to conducting the test, which are presented in Table 6.1,

TABLE 6.1 Steps to effective testing

Step 1 – Create testing KPIs

- Base your testing KPIs on your communications campaign objectives, considering what you are trying to achieve and how you will measure your success.
- Create ones which will be both useful and timely.
- Be clear about your testing KPIs from the start.
- Gain agreement/approval on your testing KPIs from the start.

Step 2 – Identify your target audience(s)

- Identify your target audience(s), both how many respondents you will require and what data you want to collect from them.
- Make sure that your target audience(s) reflects your campaign group's demographics.
- Aim for large enough sample groups from your target audience so that you can obtain reliable and meaningful information.

Step 3 – Determine your testing mechanism/methodology

- Determine if you require qualitative and/or quantitative information.
- Based on type of information required, select the appropriate mechanism/methodology (eg survey, focus group, app etc).

Step 4 – Develop your testing material

- Format your questions according to the type of information to be collected (eg quantitative or qualitative).
- Make sure that your questions, regardless of the methodology selected, are quick and easy to complete.
- Frame the questions so that they provide the specific information you require.
- Ensure that your questions are neutral and do not involve any leading questions.
- Ensure that your questions will not be seen as offensive, pushy and/or inappropriate.
- Put yourself in the shoes of your testing audience, considering how you would react if you were asked these questions.
- If possible or appropriate, ask open-ended questions to obtain more robust information.

TABLE 6.1 *Continued*

Step 5 – Consider a 'test drive'

- Consider conducting a 'test drive' (a practice test) with colleagues and/or employees to see if the test is meeting your needs/objectives.
- Be clear with those participating in test drives, explaining that this is a practice test, and not the final one.
- Ensure that the responses received in your test drive(s) provide you with the data you require.
- If you do not receive the data you require in the test drive, adjust the test as appropriate.
- Continue conducting test drives until your test is successful, and you receive appropriate and meaningful responses.

Step 6 – Analyse the information

- Pull together information in a way which will make it easy to analyse and support decision making.
- Identify categories and themes within the data.
- Look out for unintended results (information which does not fit into your original expectations).
- Do not ignore negative comments or criticism, as these can be extremely valuable.
- Keep your mind open to new ideas and/or opportunities based on the information you receive.
- Raise questions from the information (eg what does this mean, why did this occur)?
- Create a summary of the information as a way to provide high level information.
- Present detailed information in a visual manner if possible or appropriate (eg charts, graphs).

Step 7 – Update communications campaign

- Based on the findings from your test, update your communications campaign to address these requirements.
- Agree how and when you will conduct your next test.

with guidelines and suggestions to further assist you with your testing. Some of these guidelines have been highlighted previously in this chapter, and others have been added to make it a more comprehensive checklist. Keep these all in mind when preparing for and conducting your communications campaign tests.

Rating scale

An important step in developing your testing material is developing your rating scale. There has been much written on this topic as to which methodology achieves the most robust data, but the most commonly accepted methodology is the Likert 5-point scale. The Likert scale is both easy for respondents to use and lends itself to simple but powerful statistical analysis. In addition, by using this scale participants are responding to simple statements, making completion easier. Equally, once you have this type of data collected, there are a range of statistical techniques that can be applied to them to help understand the key factors you should be acting upon to improve your communications. These include correlation analysis to look at associations between questions in the data, regression analysis to help identify the key drivers of particular outcomes, and even causal path analysis so you can start predicting outcomes for the future.

Regarding the scale itself, Andy Brown, CEO of Engage, advises that it is best to use fully labelled responses so that your employees do not need to make judgements, thus limiting the impact of normative/subjective interpretation. For example, if your scale states that 1 is that you strongly disagree and 5 is that you strongly agree, it is up to individual interpretation what 2, 3 and 4 ratings mean. If on the other hand you clearly mark each rating, your employees will know exactly what each represents. This helps to ensure that the data is robust, and also assists when reporting back data. For example, if you don't clearly label the responses and report back a score of 3, you will not be able to action this score as you will not be clear as to what it means. Figure 6.2 presents some examples of the Likert 5-point scale where they have been clearly marked, and measures/returns specific attitudinal responses.

A final suggestion to make about rating scores, which is similar to other points I've made throughout the book, is that you need to create a system which will work for you and your population. For example, if you feel that a 5-point scale will be confusing and/or frustrating for your employees, then don't use it. As long as you create something which is clear and reportable, and provides you with reliable and accurate data, then again, do what is best for your communications campaign.

FIGURE 6.2 Examples of Likert 5-point scale measures

Measures agreement to question	Measures frequency of response
1. Strongly disagree	1. Very frequently
2. Disagree	2. Frequently
3. Neither agree nor disagree	3. Occasionally
4. Agree	4. Rarely
5. Strongly agree	5. Never

Measures importance of response	Measures likelihood of response
1. Very important	1. Almost always true
2. Important	2. Usually true
3. Moderately important	3. Occasionally true
4. Of little importance	4. Usually not true
5. Unimportant	5. Almost never true

Predictive analytics

To assist you further with analysing your test data, I'd like to share with you information on predictive analytics. Predictive analytics is a technique which is used to assist in analysing and mining data to paint a picture of current conditions and likely or potential futures. In respect to communications, this is extremely valuable as it helps us understand not just the current state, but what behaviours and actions our employees will take in the future depending on how we structure our communications campaign. If gives us evidence-based information by which we can develop our communications strategy and approach.

There are a variety of definitions and approaches to predictive analysis, but one which I believe explains the concept in a user-friendly manner is Andy Brown's model. His model has three levels or tiers of analytics, as shown and explained in Table 6.2.

A final point to make on this model is that you need to decide which tier will best meet your needs. Based on your communications campaign objectives, decide if you need Tier 1 analytics only, or if the addition of the more predictive levels 2 and 3 will provide more robust and informative data.

Before I end this section I'd like to point out that testing doesn't always relate to a specific communications campaign, but may be outside of a campaign. For example, you may have a pension booklet which is used as part of your day-to-day communication material. Although it is not part of

TABLE 6.2 Predictive analysis model

Tier 1 – Transactional	Tier 2 – Transitional	Tier 3 – Transformative
Descriptive tactical basics	**Insights and higher-level associations**	**Foresights and strategic priorities**
This level provides the basics and/or foundation for your analytics. It focuses on the current state, showing **relationships** between data.	This level provides insights and higher-level associations by looking at **probabilities** and **potential impacts** of the data. By doing this you can better focus on improvement.	This level involves analysing more complex data in order to predict outcomes, and provide options showing the **cause and effect** on the business. By doing this you can conduct more comprehensive ROI analytics, and focus on more transformative improvements.
Example: Testing data shows that 50% of employees prefer to receive information through an intranet site, 25% prefer to receive in written form, and 25% prefer face-to-face.	Example: Regression analysis may show that leaders communicating more openly and honestly will have twice as big an impact on employee perceptions of overall internal communications effectiveness than improving the timeliness of e-mail communications.	Example: Causal path analysis* might show that particular communication factors have a certain impact on harder business outcomes. For example: improving leadership communication may have a 10% improvement impact on talent retention; communicating your brand values more clearly to frontline employees may have a 20% improvement impact on customer satisfaction levels; and making sure that managers understand the role they can help play in your growth strategy may have a 5% improvement impact on sales.

* According to the Psychology Dictionary (www.psychologydictionary.org/causal-path), causal path analysis can be defined as a method of statistical analysis which is done by looking at correlations among variables to determine the cause and effect. Based on the pattern of correlations, it is possible to conclude which variables and in which order a path (eg attitude, behaviour, action) can be modelled from cause and effect.

a campaign, it is still important to test it from time to time to ensure that it continues to meet the needs of your employees. You can use the same testing techniques which have been explained in this chapter to track how the key drivers change over time, but the point here is that it should not be overlooked. To use an analogy, think of your communication tools as your car, which requires an annual safety inspection. This is done to ensure that your car complies with certain legal requirements and is properly maintained, which is the same for our communication tools. By testing them either during or outside of a campaign we can ensure that their effectiveness is maintained and they are in good working order.

Conclusion

In this chapter I've shared with you information on the importance and critical times to test, as well as how to effectively test. Think back to my reference to a pilot at the start of the chapter, and the important job he/she has to ensure that the plane is 'on track' and is not set up for failure along the way. In HR we need to put on our tester hat and use the techniques described in this chapter to continually collect, review and interpret the data we collect throughout testing. It may at times be a difficult and time-consuming process, but if/when we do it well we will know that our campaign is 'on track' and that we are meeting our communication campaign objectives.

To end this chapter I'd like to share with you a quote from John A Morrison, who was a famous democratic member of the US House of Representatives from Pennsylvania. He said that: 'Knowledge comes by taking things apart: analysis. But wisdom comes by putting things together'. It is our job and our responsibility to do just this, putting our data together as you would puzzle pieces to move from knowledge to wisdom. By effectively analysing and interpreting our 'puzzle pieces' we will be able to use our test data to update and refine our communications campaign based on employee feedback and insight to create the right communication pictures. And, as mentioned at the start of the chapter, we will then be able to deliver to our employees and the business a communications campaign and communication tools which are effective and are delivering an ROI to the business.

Top tips on testing

- Testing is an important step to ensure you are 'on track' for achieving your communications campaign objectives.
- Create information to demonstrate to the business the effectiveness of your communications campaign, and the ROI to the business.
- Determine up-front the type of data you require for testing (eg quantitative, qualitative) and the testing approach (eg surveys, focus groups, social media apps) which will allow you to collect the most robust data.
- Ensure that data collected through testing is useful and timely, which will then assist you in determining the effectiveness of your communications campaign.
- Use your testing data to help you make timely and appropriate changes, doing so before it is too late to influence the results and impact of your communications campaign.

Skills for being an effective tester

- A strategic mindset and approach to testing, with the ability to look at and focus on the big picture.
- An analytical mindset, with the ability to both interpret and dive deep into data.
- An inquisitive and curious nature and approach, with the ability to understand and relate the relationships between data to the business, the environment, employees etc.
- An ability to interact effectively with others so as to question and report on data and observations.
- An ability to report data in a meaningful and effective manner.

Reference

Morrison, JA [nd] http://todayinsci.com/M/Morrison_John/MorrisonJohn-Quotations.htm

Case study BT Group plc saveshare

07

Who are they?

BT Group plc (BT) is one of the world's leading providers of communications services and solutions, serving customers in more than 170 countries. Its principal activities include the provision of networked IT services globally; local, national and international telecommunications services to its customers for use at home, at work and on the move; broadband, TV and internet products and services; and converged fixed/mobile products and services. BT consists principally of five lines of business: BT Global Services, BT Business, BT Consumer, BT Wholesale and Openreach.

They have approximately 71,000 full-time equivalent employees working for the company in the UK, and around 18,000 outside the UK in 60 other countries (as at 31 March 2015).

What was the situation?

In 2009 more than 23,000 UK employees, mostly contact centre agents and engineers, joined a five-year 'saveshare' plan. The plan gives employees the opportunity to make monthly savings from net pay for a period of time. At the end of the savings period, which is called the plan maturity, employees have the choice to buy BT shares at the discounted price, or receive their money back.

The communications campaign involved the communication and engagement of these 23,000 employees at the plan maturity. With huge potential profit within their employees' reach and complex decisions to make, BT ran year-long communications to give their employees the tools and information needed to make informed choices on maturity. This was critical as employees had to consider a variety of choices including the maximization of tax allowances and reliefs and diversification.

What did they do?

The 'saveshare' maturity is thought to be one of the UK's largest broad-based employee share plan maturities ever. The communication of a complex variety of choices was a demanding challenge. Head of Employee Share Plans Francis O'Mahony said:

> There were potentially large benefits from these plans so it was even more important that people considered their choices carefully. Employees didn't get the shares automatically; to realize any potential gain, employees first had to give an instruction to buy the shares and then choose what they wanted to do with them. We wanted to make sure that participants had the right information in the right format at the right time for them to be able to make the right financial decision.

This is an extremely important point, for it highlights that in this situation if communications were not done well, employees would be impacted financially.

The BT team overcame these challenges by creating a clear and comprehensive communications strategy and campaign.

Campaign objectives

Their campaign objectives were as follows.

1. Provide sufficient information

It was critical that employees received sufficient information by which to make these important choices. BT recognized this and responded, according to Francis, by delivering their communications 'at the right place, in the right time, and through the right media'. A few examples of how they did this were:

- *Updates*: Due to the complex nature of the information, the team felt it was important to break up the information into more bite-size chunks. They did this by creating six individual updates to share with employees, each having their own theme and focus. Each included personalized details of participation, potential financial gains, tax implications, choices available, and links to the intranet maturity information portal. Examples of topics included CGT (capital gains tax), ISAs (individual savings accounts).

- *'Myth busting'*: During the campaign the team discovered that there were some myths out there, meaning employees were hearing incorrect information from others. They 'busted' these myths by creating and sharing a 'Myth-Buster' document, correcting incorrect or misleading views. Examples included information on what happened if they transferred shares into their pension, held onto their shares for five years etc.
- *'Question Time'*: The team developed and conducted a 'Question Time' audio-visual online panel chat show. This was broadcast live on the intranet site, and recorded so employees could play it back in their own time. The panel was made up of a team of internal and external experts, and answered a wide variety of questions asked by phone, online and by the audience in the auditorium.

2. Have a distinct look and feel

The BT team felt that in order to have the impact required, the communications needed to have a distinct look and feel. They did this by exploiting BT's brand developed for the plan – the distinctive and recognizable name 'saveshare', and the colour orange used in banners communicating the plan. According to Francis 'when employees saw an orange e-mail pop up they instantly knew that they needed to read it'.

3. Personalized approach

As the maturity impacted each employee in a personal way (eg number of shares, taxation etc), the team felt that it was important that communications included a personal touch and approach. They did this by sending employees personalized information to show them exactly how the maturity impacted them. An example was through sending employees personalized e- mails with links to personalized instruction pages. They also did this by creating a unique modeller, which was pre-populated with their own participation details so that they could model their own choices and calculate potential tax implications.

The communications campaign

The communications campaign included the following steps:

- *Employee survey*: Employees were invited to participate in an online survey prior to the development of the communications campaign. The purpose of the survey was to ask them what information they wanted, when and how. This provided key information by which to develop the communications campaign strategy and material.

- *E-mail updates*: Monthly e-mail updates were sent to employees in the six-month run-up to the maturity mailing. The e-mails were personalized with individual participation details and focused on different subjects. They built into a comprehensive picture of the choices available, the tax and other consequences of those choices, and where further information could be obtained.
- *E-chats*: E-chats were conducted during the instruction window. These were held so that employees could ask specific questions to understand exactly what actions they needed to take, and the consequences of each.
- *Newsdesk articles*: The BT team published interactive newsdesk articles on the BT intranet on which employees and the share plans team could post comments, providing an additional vehicle for information, as well as a means for two-way communication between employees and the BT plan experts. According to Francis this created a real buzz, increasing engagement.
- *Portal*: The BT team developed a separate portal page on the BT employee share plans intranet site because, according to Francis: 'employees were keen to see it all in one place'. The portal linked to all maturity information including copies of the updates, personalized tax modeller, maturity booklet, webchat recordings, myth buster, FAQs and presentations.
- *Helpline*: The employee share plans helpline managed by the provider, Equiniti, provided additional support to employees. The Equiniti team received extensive briefings to ensure they understood the plan, maturity and briefings available.

What did they achieve?

The key objective of the communications campaign was to provide robust and engaging information so that BT employees would take the most appropriate actions with their shares which were maturing. In addition BT wanted to raise awareness in the 'saveshare' plan in order to increase participation for the next offer. The BT team was extremely successful in achieving these objectives as shown in the following figures:

- Over 90 per cent of employees gave maturity instructions for the first maturity date (they had six months to give their maturity choices). This is evidence that employees had what they needed in order to make timely and informed decisions.

- 9 per cent more employees registered to participate in the 2014 saveshare offer. This shows that there was increased awareness, and thus great participation.
- In addition to an increase in the number of participants, the amount employees were contributing into the new plan increased. This is evidence that employees understood the value of the plan, and thus wanted to increase their participation levels.
- Feedback received from employees about the communication through the end of campaign survey was extremely positive:
  - 97 per cent were very satisfied or satisfied with the quantity and quality of the communications information.
  - 96 per cent were very satisfied or satisfied with the timeliness of information they received.
  - 94 per cent said that the amount of information received was about right to make informed choices.
  - 84 per cent found the monthly updates helpful.

What would they recommend?

Below are some top tips from the BT team based on their case study.

BT's top tips

1. Avoid jargon, especially when communicating on such a complex and technical topic as a savings-related share option plan. All it does is confuse and/or alienate employees.
2. It is important to do the 'customer journey', road-testing the employee journey and basing your communications on this. This was especially important for communicating a process, as you want employees to get the right information at the right time in the right way.
3. Be flexible in your approach to communications, reacting to feedback. We did this by adding the myth-buster in the middle of our campaign as well as posting and replying to comments to further support the sharing of knowledge.

Author's notes

I was extremely impressed with the quality and quantity of the communications material which the BT team delivered to their employees. They had a difficult challenge, balancing the need to get across complex and time-sensitive information with doing so in an engaging and non-threatening way.

Before I explain why I believe they were successful, I want to share with you feedback received from one of their employees: 'Thank you for all the communications around sharesave. They've been truly excellent. They help to make a potentially complex issue easy to understand. They've answered all of my questions and many questions I didn't even know I had.'

The BT team should be proud of such an employee reaction; I know I'd be if I received such employee feedback. What I like about the feedback, and about the communications campaign, is it shows that you can make complex communications work. By developing a robust and thoughtful strategy based on what your employees really need, you can piece together an effective communications campaign. Well done to the BT team. I definitely want you on my team next time I have to communicate on a share purchase scheme.

Case study LV= pensions

08

Who are they?

LV= is the UK's largest friendly society and a leading financial mutual, with more than 5.7 million members and customers. It insures 1 in every 10 cars in the UK, more than 800,000 homes, and is the UK's top individual income protection provider.

The company vision is to be Britain's best-loved insurer and it does this by putting its customers and employees at the heart of its business. With over 6,000 employees working in 16 offices across the UK, the positive and professional culture at LV= encourages employees to do the best they can and live by four values:

1 Treat people like family.
2 Make it feel special.
3 Know your stuff.
4 Don't wait to be asked.

These values are evident in the employee engagement activities the company has in place, and in the way it communicates with its people.

What was the situation?

The company was closing its final salary pension scheme, and needed to communicate this to the participants. The scheme had already been closed to new participants a few years ago; however, after exploring various options it was decided that the risk of such a scheme was getting too high to continue operating it effectively. At the same time, the company was inviting final salary scheme participants to join the existing defined contribution (DC) scheme, so LV= needed to communicate information on this scheme as well.

The company's concern was that these were both technical and emotional messages. If they were not communicated effectively it could have turned into an employee relations matter, and thus have a negative impact on the employees and the company.

What did they do?

A communications campaign such as this had challenges from the start, as the topic of pensions is always an emotional one, that personally impacts an employee's future. It is also a technical topic, so trying to explain the details of both the change and the new scheme presented additional challenges.

What the LV= team did well was to take the time up-front to thoroughly understand these challenges and map out a comprehensive plan to address them effectively.

Campaign objectives

Their campaign objectives were as follows.

1. Be in line with company values

One of the key values of the company is 'treat people like family'. It was critical that this message came across in the communications, making sure that employees understood why the changes were being made, and what they needed to do to make pension decisions that would work for them.

2. Be in line with company guidelines

There is a well-established 'LV= tone of voice', which can be described as conversational, easy to understand and without the use of jargon. This is easy to do for many topics, but when it comes to the technical topic of pensions, it was definitely a challenge. The LV= team worked hard to balance these guidelines with the need to present enough details for employees to understand and make key decisions.

3. Develop as a partnership

Another key way of working at LV= is through partnership, which again needed to be respected in this campaign. This presented a challenge in that such sensitive news is often not shared as companies don't want word to get out before announcements are made. The LV= team showed that you can truly partner with a wide range of colleagues to ensure the campaign is successful and still respect the confidentiality of such a project.

4. Address a diverse population

LV= has a diverse population at its 16 offices across the UK due to the various businesses in operation. This was something which needed to be addressed throughout the communications campaign. They did this by having a flexible approach to communication, keeping things as simple, clear and straightforward as possible at a high level and allowing participants to get more detail as they required on the microsite and through questions. Using the local business partners to assist in deciding what would work for their teams and offices was also important. For example, some business partners felt that a face-to-face would be needed multiple times where others felt that only one was required. This approach was effective in dealing with the needs of their diverse population.

5. Provide opportunities for two-way communication

Going back to the company value of 'treat people like family', the communications team felt that it was important to have opportunities for two-way communication with employees. This would allow employees to ask the difficult and complex questions they would have about both the change and the new scheme. They did this not only in face-to-face meetings but also through use of a question & answer forum on their dedicated project microsite.

6. Have a distinct look and feel

During the planning process the project team decided that in order for the campaign to have the impact which was required, it needed to have a distinct look and feel. It would still follow the company guidelines, but a separate brand was created so it would be recognizable to employees. A microsite within the company intranet was also created as a place to hold information and the question & answer forum which was set up for the campaign. This was also evident in that the company newsletter, which is normally used as a way to communicate, was not used, as the team felt that they wanted employees to understand that this was outside of normal communication.

7. Address employee change curve

The LV= team acknowledged that its employees would be going through a change curve with the pension changes. They worked through the various stages of change, and based their timeline on this so that employees would be ready to accept the message based on where they were on the change curve. An example is the use of personalized pension illustrations. I've seen companies send this out with the first announcement letter. The team debated this, and decided that it would be more effective to send the illustrations out after the employees had enough information to take in the illustration, as they would have advanced past the anger stage of the change curve.

The communications campaign

The communications campaign included the following steps:

- *Phase 1 Pre-consultation*: Employees who were participants of the final salary scheme were sent an e-mail, and a printed letter and brochure to their homes. The purpose of these was to inform them of the changes and invite them to join the consultation process.

  At the same time a story was posted on the company intranet so that all employees were aware of what was happening. This was an effective way of handling the situation, for, as we all know, employees talk, so best for everyone to have a general level of understanding. Finally, the pensions microsite was turned on, representing a place for information to be stored and a place to communicate with questions, thus showing a commitment to open and honest communication from the start.
- *Phase 2 Consultation/briefings*: The consultation phase lasted for three months, although legally in the UK you only need to consult for 60 days. This involved visits to 11 offices where a total of 52 briefings were conducted. They were run by one of LV='s senior executives in partnership with Peter Strudwick, Pensions Manager. According to Peter: 'We wanted our employees to know that we weren't hiding anything and had the commitment of our senior leadership team', which is why it was important to have a senior leader present at each and every session.

  I asked Peter if the briefings were difficult/challenging. He said that although there were a lot of questions, the fact that they had engaged key groups like the ECF (employee consultative forum), the pension scheme trustee and senior leaders beforehand meant the briefings went smoothly. By engaging these groups LV= were able to get them on the company's side and also present views of employees so that the management team could be prepared.

- *Phase 3 Individual statements*: A month before consultation ended, employees were sent individual statements to show them how the changes and the new scheme impacted them personally. As mentioned before, this was done separately so that employees were in the right place in the change curve to be able to engage in the process and focus on the future.

  When I asked Peter how employees reacted he said that although there was some challenge, they received less pushback than they had expected. He felt this was because of how it was communicated, with employees understanding the reason for the change due to their open, honest and respectful approach. This aligns with their value of treating employees like family, which was an important value to respect throughout the campaign.

- *Phase 4 Final communication*: The final communications material was done using the same method as the Phase 1 methodology. This was an e-mail, and a letter and brochure sent to homes, with the brochure outlining the agreed consultation outcomes. There was also an announcement on the intranet. The microsite was kept in place until the agreed scheme closure date almost a year later, with many of the key questions asked being moved to the DC scheme's new website so participants still had a record of these.

What did they achieve?

The LV= team was extremely successful in achieving the success measures they set at the start of the campaign. The first measure was to have at least 90 per cent of the final salary pension members move over to the defined contribution scheme. Due to the comprehensive approach to providing information that employees would trust and understand, 99 per cent of these employees moved to the DC scheme. They also wanted a high percentage of these employees to attend the briefing sessions so that they would have the open dialogue which they felt was important. Attendance at briefings was outstanding, with 90 per cent attending. The final measure was to protect as much as possible the employee engagement survey score. They were pleased to see that the pension change had no impact on the engagement survey, which meant that, although it was a difficult and challenging message, employees remained engaged with the company.

When I asked Peter if he felt that they had achieved their objectives he said: 'The outcomes we saw were very positive with many employees taking up enhanced pension contributions, matched by LV=. This demonstrated that they had engaged with the change.'

What would they recommend?

Below are some top tips from the LV= team based on their case study.

LV='s top tips

1. Make sure you have a strong communications plan in place, and be prepared to flex and react to it if and when it is required.
2. Be aware of the change curve when planning communications to help land your messages at the right time.
3. Be honest and empathetic when communicating to your employees. By doing this you can use 'bad news' stories to build employee trust and engagement.

Author's notes

I was impressed with the amount of thought and planning that LV= put into its communications campaign. The LV= team showed the power of understanding their audience, partnering, and creating a thoughtful and comprehensive campaign. Another area where I believe they excelled was how they kept true to their values and the objectives/guiding principles. Their values were evident in all phases of the campaign, and showed that you can effectively balance business and values. Regarding the guiding principles, they effectively created and used them throughout the campaign for all decision making, ensuring that they didn't get side-tracked. Finally, they understood and respected the employee change curve. This is absolutely critical for a communications campaign involving pensions, making the difference between success and failure. All in all it was a very professional and well-run communications campaign, and I completely understand why it has won various awards.

Case study LV= !nnovate

09

Who are they?

LV= is the UK's largest friendly society and a leading financial mutual, with more than 5.7 million members and customers. It insures 1 in every 10 cars in the UK, more than 800,000 homes, and is the UK's top individual income protection provider. For more information on LV= please refer to the previous case study on pensions.

What was the situation?

LV= was rolling out a programme which collects and recognizes employee ideas, called '!nnovate'. They previously had a programme called 'My Ideas', but felt that it needed to be improved. The new programme was developed by pulling together a team from across the business, working collaboratively to share best practices and create new ideas. They adopted a super-heroes theme for the development sessions, having everyone dress as their super-hero alter ego at the kick-off dinner. This was not only a great way for the team to informally get to know each other, but gave the sessions a 'power to the people' theme and direction for the campaign.

The result was that through shared experience and user insight the team developed !nnovate, a system which was built around a more collaborative approach to generating new business ideas. This move to collaboration was evident in many ways. First of all, through the name, moving away from the title of 'my' idea. It was also evident in how the system worked, for once employee ideas were posted on the system others could see it, like it and progress it forward. This was possible as the system was built on a social media platform, providing the functionality which encourages collaboration.

What did they do?

The !nnovate programme was first piloted in September 2014 to about 60 per cent of LV='s employee population, with the final programme officially launched in July 2015.

Campaign objectives

The objectives of LV='s !nnovate communications campaign were as follows.

1. Generate excitement

A challenge of the communications campaign was that they were moving away from a legacy programme to a new one. They needed to find a way to generate excitement about the new programme, conveying the message to employees that this was something new, exciting and something which they really should learn more about. Going back to the point made in Chapter 5 about WIIFM (what's in it for me?), LV= needed to communicate to their employees that this new programme would be better for them personally.

One example of how LV= addressed this was through their pre-launch creation of a 'community' through social media. Employees were invited to join the community, and by doing so were able to view and comment. The size of the community tripled in size based on word of mouth, thus creating interest and excitement before the programme was even launched. What this meant was that by the time the official communications campaign began, there was already excitement and anticipation from employees. This is an illustration of how informal communication, which in this case was word of mouth, can have a powerful impact on more formal communication campaigns.

2. Explain new technology

The power of the new programme was that it was designed by the people and for the people. It was built internally using open source technology, allowing it to be extremely engaging in how it worked. However, not all employees at LV= (or at any other company) understand and/or are excited by technology, and the use of social media platforms. For this reason, a challenge of the communications campaign was to balance the needs of these two diverse populations – those that were extremely familiar with social media and those that were not comfortable and possibly intimidated by social media.

The LV= team addressed this by creating a variety of user-friendly tools and material to clearly explain how to use the system. They used traditional tools such as a brochure, FAQs and webinars, as well as creating an interactive video learning tool. This video tool was developed so that employees could learn how to use the system 'in their own time', being able to stop and start the video as they learned how to navigate through the new system. This is a brilliant example of a non-threatening communications vehicle, working well for those intimidated by technology.

3. Address diverse population

LV= had a variety of diversity challenges to overcome in their communication campaign. The first was based on the diversity of their business and geography, having 16 offices across the UK operating in a variety of businesses. The second challenge was the challenge of those that were comfortable with technology, and those that were not (discussed above). And the final challenge was that there were some employees involved in the pilot and others who were not. The team needed to communicate to these populations in different ways, as they needed and wanted different information.

The LV= team addressed these diversity challenges in the following ways:

- *Flexibility*: To address the first challenge of multiple locations and businesses, the LV= project team incorporated flexibility into the design of their communications campaign. This allowed each location/business to decide if/when they wanted to make use of some of the communication vehicles such as face-to-face workshops, webinars etc. This ensured that the individual communication needs were addressed in a flexible manner. This was not only effective, but was appreciated by business leaders, being another win for the communications campaign.
- *Multiple media*: I previously explained how LV= handled the challenge of engaging employees who were comfortable with technology and those who were not. They did this by using a variety of media (eg print, digital and live) to create user-friendly tools. This assisted in overcoming the challenge of different knowledge bases, and also the challenge of different preferences in receiving information. What this relates to is that different people like to receive information in different ways. As explained earlier in the book, this can be based on differences based on generation, situation, culture etc.

As LV= used such a multitude of media, they were able to address the needs of each of these groups, doing so in a comprehensive and creative way.

- *Segmentation*: To handle the third challenge of having different audiences (those who were part of the pilot and those who were not), LV= segmented some of their communications. They did this so that the content was valuable and relevant to each population, which goes back to the guiding principles of communication. It focused the employee on what they needed to know, and what actions they needed to take.

4. Have a distinct look and feel

The team wanted it to be very clear to employees that this was a new programme, and that it should be noticed. They did this by creating communication material which had a distinct look and feel, having it stand out. They created a slightly comic book approach to their communications, doing so in the words and graphics which were used. According to Kim Ewin-Hill, Business Technologist and !nnovate Business Systems Owner, CIO: 'We tried to make it a bit more special to our employees. We didn't want it to be seen as another business tool, but something which was personal to them.' They were able to balance the fun of the communications with corporate guidelines, creating something with a distinct look and feel. The picture in Figure 9.1 was taken from one of the communication documents, and illustrates this look and feel.

The communications campaign

The communications campaign included the following:

- *Brochures*: A brochure was created as a way to explain the new programme, both in what it was and how it was different from the previous programme. It followed the super-hero theme, which was 'giving power to the people'. The brochure was effective in balancing the need for information and the need to present a strong, recognizable brand. This worked well in engaging employees in the new programme. Figure 9.2 shows two example pages from the brochure.
- *Series of news stories*: As part of the communications launch, monthly news stories were put onto the programme's intranet site. The purpose was to provide information and updates, and

FIGURE 9.1 LV= !nnovate campaign: look and feel

FIGURE 9.2 Pages from the !nnovate brochure

A

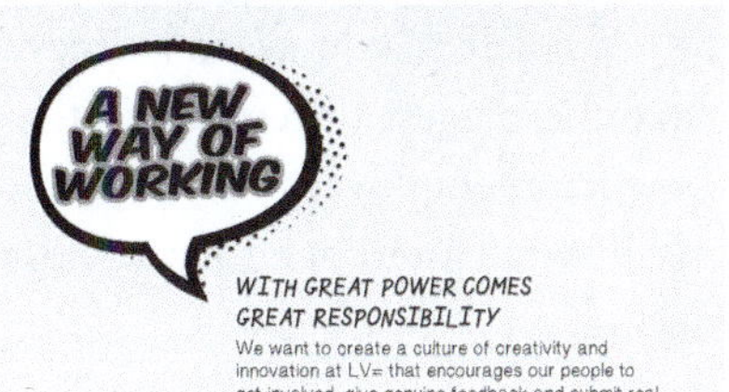

B

also to act as a way to continually engage employees with the programme. This is a great example of keeping the momentum going during a communications campaign. It was also effective in driving employees to the intranet site, creating a better chance of them using the new system.

- *Company-wide magazine articles*: The LV= team made use of an existing communications vehicle, which was their company-wide magazine. They had a separate section of the magazine created for the !nnovate programme, using it to share employee success stories with the programme. This was yet another way to create interest and engagement. It also follows an approach I mentioned earlier in the book about looking at what already exists before creating new communication vehicles.
- *Presentations to executives*: The LV= team went around to monthly executive meetings to present on the !nnovate programme as part of the communications campaign. They tailored the presentations for each business, giving examples specific to their area. This was done so that the execs felt a part of and supported the campaign and the programme. According to Kim, it was a great way to get them involved, which (as mentioned in the chapter about Allies) is critical to the success of the campaign and its objectives.
- *Stands at events*: The LV= team felt that it was important to include a personal touch as part of their communications campaign, and thus had an !nnovate stand at various manager and employee events. They used this as a way to meet face to face with employees to answer their questions and create excitement and engagement in the programme.

What did they achieve?

The success measures for the communications campaign were to raise awareness of the new programme, increase collaboration and increase utilization. You'll notice that utilization was the last objective listed. This was because the team felt that it wasn't necessarily the number of ideas which would make the biggest difference to the business. The biggest differences would come from employees who understood how the programme worked, and a collaborated approach to generating great ideas. Their achievements were as follows:

- Data from the system showed that 11 per cent of employees go onto !nnovate daily, meaning they go onto it and actively either generate ideas or vote on ideas. Another 17 per cent of employees go onto !nnovate weekly. These usage rates exceed the norm for such programmes, and are evidence of how the communications campaign raised both awareness and utilization.
- Collaboration between employees is evident through the number and quality of new ideas which have been implemented since the programme was launched. Employees have clearly understood how to use the system to work together to generate ideas, using the social media platform through !nnovate as a way to share and vote on ideas.
- The time it takes to implement a new idea has been reduced by 55 days, which is a fantastic achievement. What this means is that employees not only understand how to effectively use the programme, but through collaboration ideas are more quickly implemented.

What would they recommend?

Below are some top tips from the LV= team based on their case study.

LV= !nnovate's top tips

1. Establish clear links to business goals and 'sell the story'. Projects that can seem 'non-critical' on the surface can become true enablers of critical business objectives by drawing out the links clearly and concisely through your communications campaign.
2. Don't underestimate the importance of a supportive and passionate project team, members who will put employee needs at the forefront of all decisions.
3. Don't be afraid to refine your approach. It is important to review the success of your communications at key milestones, and not be afraid to revisit or revise your plan/approach. If you do this, in the long term your project will have a greater chance of success.

Author's notes

I was impressed with the creative and comprehensive manner in which the LV= team designed and delivered their communications campaign. Just the name of the programme alone (!nnovate) is creative, communicating to their employees from the beginning that this was not just another programme or message. They were brave in the way in which they communicated (I loved the comic book approach) as well as the number and diversity of tools they created. I'm sure this took a lot of time and dedication to develop and get right, but as you can see from their results, it was definitely worth it as they achieved all of their objectives.

The other area where I believe they were role models is in respect to how they partnered with their allies. They did this throughout the campaign in a variety of ways. The first way was by creating and engaging with their project team (I loved how they had the team come to their kick-off meeting dressed as super-heroes). The next way was by using the social media community as a way to reach and engage with a wider group of employees. Finally, they took the time to visit many of the offices to meet with execs, managers and employees to explain the programme and gain their support. These actions illustrate how helpful it can be to develop and maintain allies throughout a communications campaign, doing so in a comprehensive manner.

Overall I believe that LV='s communications campaign was effective in being able to engage the business and employees with their updated programme. It is often easier to communicate a new programme, with employees eager to learn more about it. However, LV= showed that if you get your communications right, you can also create eagerness and excitement for an updated programme.

Case study Merlin Entertainments

10

Who are they?

Merlin Entertainments is the second largest leisure business in the world, and the team behind some of the best-known names in global leisure. These include SEA LIFE, Madame Tussauds, the Dungeons and LEGOLAND, as well as icons such as The London Eye, Sydney Tower Eye and SKYWALK, Blackpool Tower, Gardaland Resort, Heide Park Resort and Alton Towers Resort. They operate 106 attractions in 23 countries across four continents, and have 27,000 employees.

What was the situation?

The company wanted to rejuvenate and recommunicate their employer brand, which centres around their values – The Merlin Way. The Merlin Way had been integral to their business since its conception in 2011, and following their IPO in 2013 they were seeking a way to refresh the branding of their values: Merlin's employee research showed that the Merlin Way is the primary factor that impacts employee engagement. It further identified that they needed a broader vision on how they were communicated.

They looked at this in more detail really thinking about 'What makes Merlin different? What makes Merlin special? What makes Merlin – well, Merlin?' Looking at their competitors they differentiated themselves with the FUN element – the FUN memories they provide. This led to Merlin really looking at the WHAT, HOW & WHY model (Figure 10.1).

FIGURE 10.1 The Merlin 'What, How & Why' model

This led to the development of the concept of FOR THE LOVE OF FUN (FTLOF), placing everything they did at the heart of the new Merlin Way (Figure 10.2):

> The Merlin Way is integral to how we operate – injecting capital letters FUN into everything we do. The Merlin Way originated as a set of values and developed into a wheel, all around the delivery of memorable experiences. This year we took it further by placing FUN at the heart. If our employees are having FUN this will translate to our customers. So it's ALL FOR THE LOVE OF FUN (FTLOF)!
>
> Tea Colaianni, Group Human Resources Director

FIGURE 10.2 The Merlin FTLOF campaign

What did they do?

Merlin developed a very creative and comprehensive communications strategy and campaign, with the aim of embedding the new Merlin Way and FTLOF throughout the whole employee life cycle.

Campaign objectives

Some of the key objectives of the campaign were as follows.

1. Creation of engaging tools

As the Merlin business is about people and creating memorable experiences for their visitors, it was important that the communications were engaging and memorable to their employees. They did this by creating and integrating the newly created FUN brand, utilizing not only a wide variety of media but ones that were extremely creative. Examples of these engaging tools were:

- FUN box: this was a creative and quality item which was created and presented as a special gift to each senior leader as a way to cascade the messages to their teams. The box contained a film to be used to introduce the campaign, as well as other tools which each attraction could use as they wish to launch the campaign.
- FUN goggles: these were an innovative tool used as a gimmick to illustrate how employees needed to look at their business, looking into a FUN new world (Figure 10.3).
- FUN'O'METER: this was a creative and unique way which was created to encourage employees to embrace FUN, trying to get a higher fun value in how they behaved and what they did. Scores ranged from a low 'mouth twitch' to a high 'real tears', with the other fun categories being 'wide smile', 'little giggle' and 'belly laugh' (Figure 10.4).

FIGURE 10.3 The Merlin FUN goggles

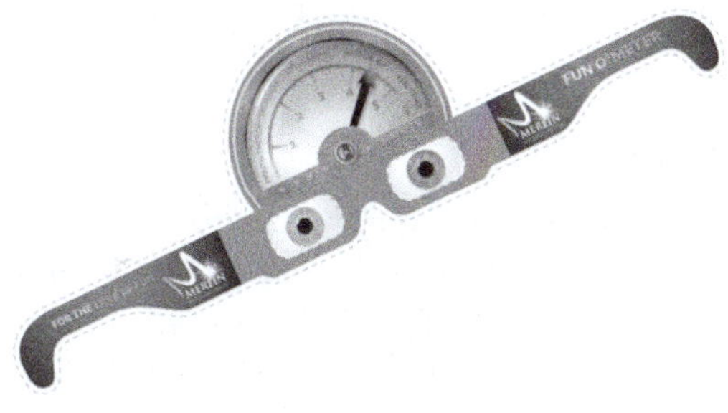

FIGURE 10.4 The Merlin FUN'O'METER

2. Creation of something different

In order to grab the attention and engage employees in the communications campaign, the style of presentation and tone of voice used were different to anything that had been done before. They did this by creating crisp impactful visuals to tell the story with short, sharp copy to bring things to life. They ditched 'corporate', formal jargon and injected informality, fun and humour in their written communication. Not only was the content done differently, but as mentioned previously, different tools and media were used.

3. Adoption of a flexible approach

Global guidelines and tools were developed, and each attraction was given flexibility to determine how best to launch the campaign. The attraction HR representative worked with the business leaders to decide what would work best for their business and their employees. An example is at LEGOLAND Windsor, where they launched a teaser campaign, letting employees know that something FUN was coming by putting balloons on employee cars along with an invite to say the FUN is coming. Another example was at LEGOLAND California, where they created and recruited for their 'FUN squad', having employees interview to play this role throughout the campaign.

4. Use of global tools

As Merlin is a global organization they needed to have communication tools that could be shared across their businesses in 23 countries, incorporating language and cultural variances. They did this in the following ways:

- Created tools that worked effectively in all countries.
- Translated material into 15 different languages.
- Organized regional and local WebExs to fit with the various time zones.
- Put all material on the HR 'Spell Point', a global document depository, so that all HR business partners not only had access but could share ideas using this global tool.

The communications campaign

The communications campaign included the following steps:

- *Presentation*: An initial presentation with video was given at the annual global strategy conference for the top 80 leaders. This was done so that the senior leaders were aware and engaged with the concepts and campaign from the start.
- *Global WebEx*: A global WebEx was conducted for the global HR community. This was done so that they, like senior leaders, were aware and engaged. In addition, it also ensured that the HR team could begin thinking of how best to roll out the communications campaign in each of their local attractions.
- *Global launch*: The campaign was launched at the global HR conference to the global HR community. HR business partners were fully briefed on the campaign, their role, and given the material.
- *Individual launch*: Each individual attraction launched the campaign to their employees using the global concepts and tools. They launched it in their own unique way, selecting the most impactful and engaging approach.

What did they achieve?

The aim of the communications campaign was very bold, not only introducing FTLOF into their company values, but asking the business to approach everyday activities from a different perspective. Over the last twelve months they have already seen changes based on the impactful communications campaign. They have examples of how attractions have injected FUN into what they do, from simple examples of writing e-mails with a FUN tone of voice, to including FUN activities in normal events (eg they had a contest to see how fast employees could eat a chocolate Easter egg to try to win a world record at a recent meeting).

Another aim of the communications campaign was to increase the employee engagement score from the employee survey. This was a challenge as engagement is already extremely high at Merlin. However, they were successful in doing so through their effective programme and communications campaign.

According to Tea Colaianni, Group Human Resources Director: 'Our attractions across the globe have engaged and come up with fabulous ways of embedding FUN into everything. Our values are unique and being part of Team Merlin we believe in the delivery of FUN memorable experiences being at the heart of everything we do!' Our employee engagement scores have jumped up in the 90s – 96 per cent of an employees say they enjoy working at Merlin. The Merlin Way is a driver of our employees' engagement.

What would they recommend?

Here are some top tips from the Merlin team based on their case study.

1. Be true to your overall objectives, putting these at the heart of everything you do in your communications campaign.
2. Create messages which are consistent and clear to ensure that you are communicating the what, why and how so that you get the right messages across to your employees.
3. Create messages that can be received at a global level, understanding and respecting the global differences
4. Ditch the corporate speak and embrace the fun.

Author's notes

What I really like about this case study is the creativity which was used throughout the campaign. Yes, you would expect communication in this industry to be creative, but I believe that Merlin went above and beyond in the world of creativity. The branding (FTLOF) itself was so catchy, creating an impactful theme to use throughout the campaign. And how could you not love FUN goggles or a FUN'O'METER? What a great way to creatively get a message and change of behaviours across to the business and employees.

The other thing I'd like to point out from this case study is the 'stickiness' of the campaign. I used this term earlier in the book, citing how important it is to make our messages stick with our employees. Merlin did this brilliantly as their messages and tools were developed to be used during and after the communications campaign, embedding them in how they act and operate as a business. Well done to Merlin for creating such an amazing communications campaign. I only have one question for them. Can I please have a pair of FUN goggles?

Case study Reward Gateway Project Solar

11

Who are they?

Reward Gateway provides employee engagement technology. Over 1,100 clients use the company's products to attract, engage and retain the best employees. The company's products power employee communications, employee recognition and employee benefits through a single employer-branded hub called SmartHub. They have approximately 300 employees working in six offices across five countries.

What was the situation?

The company was at an interesting time in their evolution as a leading employee engagement technology specialist. They were finishing a cycle of investment with one investor (Inflexion), and were beginning to look for their next private equity investor. For most companies this would be a straightforward communications process, communicating to/with potential investors using 'normal' tools and processes, and communicating to employees only when the deal had been made. However, at Reward Gateway 'normal' is not in their vocabulary, and thus began Project Solar, which included a communications campaign that was both unique and effective.

What did they do?

From a communications perspective, Project Solar had two key audiences: external potential investors and internal employees. A challenge of this campaign was balancing communicating the critical business and legal requirements with communicating in a way that fit the culture and personality of Reward Gateway.

Campaign objectives

The objectives of the communications campaign were as follows.

1. Take it slowly

According to Glenn Elliott, Founder and CEO: 'Being in a position to choose your investor is a great position to be in, and quite a burden! It's a huge decision and will form the basis of the next five or so years of the business. So like all really important decisions we took it slowly.'

They did this by embarking on a nine-month process which involved communicating the right information, at the right time and in their own unique way. By going slowly and thoughtfully they were able to meet their overall business objectives of selecting the right investor, and thoroughly engaging their employees along the way.

2. Tell the Reward Gateway 'story'

It was important for Reward Gateway to find their next investor, but it had to be the right investor. The investor had to understand and embrace who they were, understand their vision for employee engagement, as well as their clients and employees. Being dedicated to an honest, transparent, clear and simple business model, Reward Gateway designed their external communications campaign to explain and show this through telling investors their story, both past and future.

They told this story through the normal IM (information memorandum), which is a document providing an overview of the company to potential buyers. However, they didn't feel that this was enough, so they created the following two additional 'chapters' to their story:

- The first 'chapter' was what they called their 'alternative IM'. It was a beautiful coffee-table book they had created to tell the story of Reward Gateway through a professional photo archive they had been building up for the last five years. It had the subtitle 'Because we're human', and included chapters explaining their product and their people in a very personal way. The book was effective in using pictures and words to engage potential investors as only a story book can.

- The second 'chapter' was a video IM which was produced in-house. It brought the Reward Gateway story further to life, through interviews and conversations with employees about products, and with clients about their experiences. It also contained video clips from their own internal employee communication videos, showing the human side of the business. As only a video can, it took the words and gave them further meaning, connecting potential investors to the company and their people.

Although it was not a physical 'chapter', another way that they told their story to potential investors was in how they managed their investor meetings. Instead of holding them hidden away in boardrooms or off site, they met every single investor in their open-plan office. As Glenn described it to me: 'We perched them on the sofas in the cafe of our London headquarters and let them roam freely to talk to any of our people on their visits. We encouraged as much contact as possible because we wanted them to see how well everyone got on.' What a great way to show the potential investors the real Reward Gateway!

3. Remove the fear from the unknown

The Reward Gateway leadership team felt it was important to have constant engagement at every stage of the process with their employees. This was so that employees would be genuinely excited to be a part of the next step in the company's journey, and to remove the fear from the unknown for their employees. Another key reason is because all employees are shareholders through their employee share scheme, and thus this project (and the outcome) had another element of personal impact on them.

They removed this fear in two effective ways. The first was to demystify the events, meaning they communicated in a way which made a difficult subject clearer and easier to understand. The second was to keep their employees informed at every stage of the process through a variety of update mechanisms which I'll explain in the next section.

4. Maintain trust

Trust is a cornerstone of the relationship Reward Gateway has with its employees, and a strong part of its culture. According to Tracy Mellor (Group People Director and Managing Director Australia and New Zealand): 'Very little is secret and confidential within Reward Gateway. Our general approach is to trust all RG people and empower them with knowledge – whether the news is good or bad.' For this reason, the communications throughout the project needed to contain the 'normal' amount of open, honest and transparent messages which all employees expected.

They did this by using a variety of update mechanisms throughout the process, all working together to provide timely and open information and messages. These ensured that employees were connected to what was happening, and how the project was progressing.

5. Manage talent

Key to the Reward Gateway business was/is their employees, so maintaining this talent was critical. According to Shelley Packer, Director of Global Communications, 'We wanted employees to stay for 'Season Three' as it became known. We wanted to see sparkly-eyed people planning their future with us.' For this reason they built into their communications strategy and campaign ways to inspire employees to 'join the journey', staying around for the next five-year investment cycle (the next 'season'). One way they did this was by communicating the opportunities for the company and them personally that this new chapter presented. Branding it as 'what will you be doing in five years?', the CEO made a presentation at one of their global business updates (GBU) where he shared actual stories of how employees had progressed over the previous five-year cycle. This illustrated what had happened in the last cycle, giving employees motivation to stay around for the next round of opportunities. Watching the film, employees were inspired to see where their future at Reward Gateway may lead them, and hopefully see their picture and story on the screen in the next five years. This was a creative and effective way of getting a point across, engaging and inspiring employees for the future.

The communications campaign

The communications campaign for the employee communication elements included the following:

- *Global Briefings*: Global Briefings, which are Reward Gateway's fortnightly update 'meetings', were used as a communications tool throughout the process. The in-house TV programmes are filmed every Friday and sent to all global locations to view at 9.00 am on the Monday. They are fun and bouncy most of the time, but they are also used as a way to break big news. This was the case with Project Solar, for which it was used throughout the process as a way to provide regular updates on timings and activities. According to

Shelley Packer, 'it let everyone know what was going on in the basement', which is where the leadership were meeting much of the time working on the project.

- *Global Business Updates*: Global Business Updates (GBU) are an absolute cornerstone of their open and honest communications culture as well. It is their quarterly 'all hands' employee conference which is filmed live and streamed to all global locations, thus ensuring that messages are received at the same time. It is a normal and expected way to communicate to employees, and for this reason was used to provide information and updates throughout the process. They did this in their own unique way, using videos to depict what was going on at various key times (see next point).
- *Videos*: Reward Gateway used videos throughout the campaign as a way to communicate to both potential investors and employees. The videos had a reality TV feel about them as they followed the leadership team throughout the process, clearly explaining things in an open and honest manner. Examples of these were:
  - 'The man behind the suit' video: this video contained 90-second videos with potential investors, acting as a way to remove fear by showing investors as people and not just names. As Glenn explained to me, it showed 'people just doing a job'.
  - 'Meet the investor' video: this second video was shown to employees to announce the completion of Project Solar. The objective was to announce the new investor (Great Hill Partners LLP), and to share the vision for the next five years working alongside the new investor. According to Shelley Packer: 'The purpose of this video was to share the human side of the investors. We wanted employees to be able to visualize and connect with the new investors.' This was done by interviewing members of the new investor team, having them candidly talk about who they were and why they were excited to be working with the company. The ending was poignant as the CEO announced the new investor outside the office where the company first began.
- *Engagement hub*: Another existing communication vehicle which was used throughout the communications campaign was Boom!, which is their employee engagement hub using their own SmartHub® technology. They created a separate section within this hub which contained up-to-date information/updates, questions and answers, and a blog written by CEO Glenn Elliott. This was effective in

bringing all of the important information together in one place, making it easily accessible to employees in an engaging manner.

- *Social media*: Being a technology company with a young and global workforce, social media is an accepted and expected communications medium. So for this communications campaign Reward Gateway used all social media channels (eg Instagram, Twitter, Facebook). They used them all, not selecting one over another, as it was felt that since everyone has their preferred channel they should all be used. This was effective in keeping communications two-way, helping to remove the fear of the process, and engaging employees along the way.
- *Personalized share letters*: One of the key messages throughout the communications campaign was that all employees with three or more years' service would benefit as part of this investment cycle through the employee share ownership plan. In the final announcement video the CEO announced that the plan was paying out to each and every employee, regardless of when they joined the company. He went on to say that personalized share letters would be available to download that same day, so that there would be no questions as to what employees were receiving. Although this took a lot of work to prepare so quickly, the company felt that it further communicated their commitment to an open, honest and fair way of working with their employees.

What did they achieve?

The key objectives of the communications campaign were to select the 'right' investor, to remove the mystery and fear from such an event for their employees, and to retain their key talent. The Reward Gateway team was extremely successful in achieving these objectives:

- They achieved their objective of entering into a partnership with the 'right' investor, Great Hill Partners LLP. The deal was 'right' as it will fuel the expansion of products and technology, and will fund geographic expansion outside of the company's current markets. Just as important, they are 'right' as they truly understand and appreciate Reward Gateway's culture and business model thanks to the effective communication vehicles they used.

  As Chris Busby, Partner at Great Hill Partners LLP, said on a GBU video: 'Reward Gateway's incredibly unique communication products helped us understand their business in a way most companies don't normally do.'

- They kept their employees informed throughout the process, ensuring they were clear as to what was happening. They did a survey at the end of the GBU where they announced the new investor: 95 per cent said that they felt more connected to and understood the business better at the end of the process; 92.7 per cent said they understood the decisions the leadership team made throughout the process; and finally, 92.7 per cent said they felt informed about what was happening overall.
- They were able to retain their key staff, setting them up for the future. According to Tracy Mellor: 'Before the sale we identified a group of 35 people we considered "key talent" who we thought may be at risk of leaving after they received their share money and we took action to protect them. Now, a couple of months on we have retained all but one of them.'

What would they recommend?

Below are some top tips from the Reward Gateway team based on their case study.

Reward Gateway's top tips

1. Be honest with your employees; they can handle it. If you hide things from them they will only make up their own story, and it's often a lot more dramatic than the reality.
2. Remember that the purpose of communication is to create ACTION. Before you start any campaign, clearly write what action(s) you want to see, and make sure that your plan supports these goals.
3. Don't forget to give employees the opportunity to give feedback. A tip we used was to advertise the survey during employee downtime (eg on the way to work, lunchtime, journey home), as you'll get a higher response rate.
4. If you have a communications campaign which will take place over a period of time, consider the communication needed to get your new employees up to speed with the story. This ensures that they get the full story, and not just the ending.

Author's notes

I was extremely impressed with Reward Gateway's approach to handling their communications campaign. They used courage in how they dealt with both potential investors and employees, using their own unique and engaging way to show investors who they were and bring their employees along on the journey. I say that they used courage, as often in these situations things are done in quite a secretive manner, with employees either not knowing anything or guessing what is happening around them. How can this be seen as open and honest communication? Also, with investors, how can they know who they are investing in if they are shown just a traditional IM? Reward Gateway showed that being transparent builds trust, cooperation and engagement.

Another area which impressed me was their use of existing communication channels and media. Often we jump in and create new ways to communicate for our campaigns, but with such an established and effective communications strategy and approach in place, why, as the expression goes, 'reinvent the wheel'? If it works, use it!

My final note points out how Reward Gateway went above and beyond what is normally done and expected in such a situation. With the amount of work involved with the reinvestment process the Reward Gateway team could have done just what was expected of them. But they didn't; they did so much more, creating documents, videos etc, which I'm sure were time-consuming but oh so effective. They shared with me the videos and the alternative IM, and I could see first-hand the effort and care put into these. Well done to the Reward Gateway team for turning a routine exercise into an exciting experience for all involved. I wonder what they will do in another five years when it's time for the next round of investments?

Conclusion

12

We've come to the end of the book, a time when we reflect on what we've learned, and bring it all together. In this chapter we will cover the following:

- Summary of IMPACT model.
- Winning attitude.
- Final words of wisdom.
- Happy ending.

Summary of IMPACT model

As mentioned throughout this book, the aim of effective communication is to create a shared meaning and a call to action. By doing this, your communications can assist you and your business in achieving the key objectives shown in Figure 12.1.

The IMPACT model which I've shared with you throughout the book will assist you in achieving these objectives. The key points to keep in mind when using the model are:

- *The steps are non-sequential*: All steps in the model should be done in a fluid and flexible manner. Work with your team to carry them out at the right time using a joined up approach.

FIGURE 12.1 Key reasons for communications

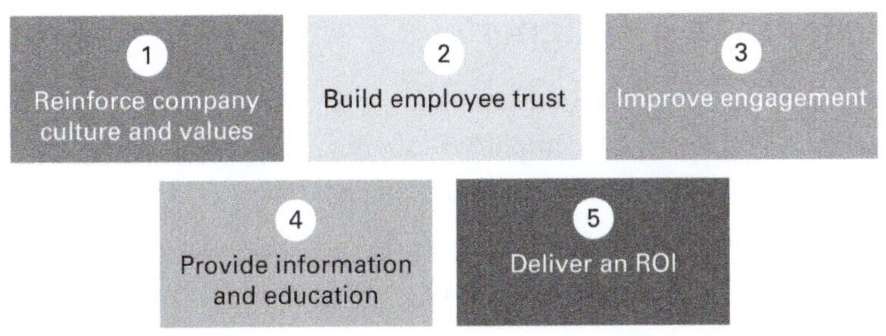

- *All steps should be taken*: It is important to take all steps in the model, and not skip over them in haste or in error. This ensures that everything has been considered and actioned in an effective manner.
- *Keep your focus*: Always go back to your communication objectives, keeping these in mind as you develop and deliver your communications campaign. If something is not in line with your objectives, question whether it makes sense to be done.
- *Wear your 'hat'*: When carrying out the work in each step, put on your 'hat'. This will help you and your team focus on the skills and actions required to complete the step effectively.

As explained in each chapter, each step of the IMPACT model has unique actions and objectives. The key points from each chapter and for each step are summarized here.

1. *Investigation: be a* detective

- Take the time for investigation, remember that you can't 'solve the crime' without the facts.
- Cultivate an eye for detail, asking the right questions of the right people.
- Look, listen and smell the 'crime scene', making sure you haven't missed any important clues.
- Be objective and analytical, using data to help you reach your conclusions.
- Revisit the 'crime scene', going back and checking and rechecking your facts and the data.
- Develop robust objectives that are clear and deliver achievable ROI to the business.

2. *Medium: be a* designer

- Select medium/media that have the right 'fit' for your organization and communications campaign – aligning with your objectives, your culture, your audience and your timelines.
- Understand the benefits of each medium, selecting those where the advantages will meet the needs of your communications campaign.

- Ensure that you have taken into consideration what each medium can and cannot achieve, and how this fits into your overall objectives and calls to action.
- Understand how the ever-increasing use of digital media will or will not work at your organization, using those that work best with your organization from a culture and technology perspective.

3. *Planning: be a* project manager

- Have agreed objectives, deliverables and timelines determined and agreed up-front.
- Create a coordinated and collaborative approach to working with your project team and stakeholders.
- Be clear about responsibilities and how decisions are to be made.
- Address and manage tasks, issues and risks honestly and effectively.
- Adopt a flexible and adaptable approach to be able to handle all circumstances.

4. *Allies: be a* campaigner

- By working with allies you have more 'power' and can expand your pool of resources.
- Working with allies is a two-way street – they help you and you help them.
- Take the time up-front to develop strong relationships with your allies.
- Clearly define to your allies their role, what's in it for them, and set expectations.
- Keep the lines of communication open between you and your allies.

5. *Content: be a* writer

- Create content which will make your messages stick, creating the 'stickiness' that will make your employees read it over and over again.
- Create content which will encourage your employees to read, think and behave differently.
- Follow the guiding principles of content, which are to create valuable, relevant and consistent content.

- Create words and graphics which are simple to understand and associate with, and link to your key messages.
- Determine if/when segmentation would be helpful in ensuring that your content is appropriate to your different employee groups.
- Consider the multi-generational workforce when creating content – what is their 'sphere of influence' which they will refer to when taking in communications content.
- Consider how your content will work with global audiences, and whether you need to adapt to ensure it is effective globally.

6. *Testing: be a* tester

- Create information to demonstrate to the business the effectiveness of your communications campaign, and the ROI to the business.
- Determine up-front the type of data you require for testing (eg quantitative, qualitative) and the testing approach (eg surveys, focus groups, social media, apps) which will allow you to collect the most robust data.
- Ensure that data collected through testing is useful and timely, which will then assist you in determining the effectiveness of your communications campaign.
- Use your testing data to help you make timely and appropriate changes, doing so before it is too late to influence the results and impact of your communications campaign.

Winning attitude

Ask anyone who's worked with me, and they will say that I start out every communications campaign asking the question: 'What do we need to do to win an award?' I do this partly because I have a (very) competitive personality, but also because I know that by setting this as a goal we will:

- set meaningful and challenging objectives;
- select and develop award-winning media and content;
- build a strong project team and partnerships;
- create test measures which will give meaning to the campaign;
- do what is right for the company in order to deliver the greatest ROI.

But is this enough; will this help you win an award? Often yes, but sometimes you need something which Lisa Turnball (Communications Manager at Reward Gateway) describes as a little 'magic'. I like to think of this as a secret ingredient you add to your communications mix, something which will push the boundaries, making it something which your employees will never forget.

Lisa shared with me a few examples of what she has done with her clients to illustrate this concept. The first example was a 'magic mirror', which was something they used in company rest rooms. How it worked was that they put sensors in the mirrors so that a message appeared when the employee stood in front of the mirror. The message was kept simple and to the point, while the visuals were bright and eye-catching. Together they were effective in meeting the core objective, which was to attract people to use the newly launched employee portal. It was something which was unexpected, and definitely made the employees take notice. Another example was when they put LED lights in posters which were hung throughout the offices. The lights created more attention to the poster, encouraging employees to stop and take notice. Both show how a little magic can engage your employees in the message, giving you an extra tool by which to achieve your objectives. If you want a few more inspirational 'magic' ideas, Merlin Entertainments used some very creative ones (fun goggles, fun barometer) which are explained in their case study on page 199.

Final words of wisdom

Throughout the book I've provided tips, tools and words of wisdom such as the ones just shared. To be sure that you have as many practical and helpful tips as possible, I'd like to share a few more with you. These final words of wisdom come from some of my team of fantastic contributors:

> Our research suggests that a commitment to transparency, a clear reward communications plan and a well-resourced, multi-media and two-way approach are what differentiates the successful employers from the rest.
>
> Duncan Brown, Head of HR Consultancy, Institute for Employment Studies

> In the social media-savvy world we live in the old style top-down one-way 'tell' communications is thankfully on its way out. How we engage with staff and other stakeholders is critical. It touches upon emotions including 'what I'm worth, what my manager and company think I'm worth' etc.
>
> Sylvia Doyle, founder and Managing Consultant of Reward First® People Consulting

> Linking the branding and imagery used in a communications strategy to an organization's external brand and business activities can really help to engage staff with these.
>
> Debbie Lovewell-Tuck, editor of *Employee Benefits*

> When communicating, always check that your audience understands you. If they don't, then adapt and try again. It is your job to make them understand, not their job to untangle what you said.
>
> Debi O'Donovan, founder of Reward & Employee Benefits Association

> Communicating with employees has never been more important – or so contended. The best HR communications will learn from digital and offline marketing, behavioural psychology and use clever generational and regional insights to target and build the best engagement techniques for their particular workforce audience.
>
> Alex Thurley-Ratcliff, Head of Research and Development, SHILLING, an Arthur J Gallagher company

I'd like to thank these contributors, as well as all of the others who have contributed throughout the book. You have all been wonderful! You not only contributed through the information, examples and quotes included in the book, but you also acted as a sounding board and partner for developing my own thoughts and ideas. This has made the book a much more comprehensive and robust tool, which I hope will assist my fellow HR professionals as you begin your next communications campaign.

Happy ending

Every book needs a happy ending. For you, my hope is that your happy ending is to develop and deliver effective communication campaigns. My other hope is that you enjoy working on these campaigns as much as I enjoy doing so, feeling comfortable that you have the knowledge and tools to be effective. All the best in being the winner that I know you can be!

Regarding my personal happy ending, I achieved this by meeting my goal of writing this book, learning so much personally along the way. I also had a surprise happy ending as a direct result of writing this book, and that was to find a new and exciting job as Group Reward Director at Reward Gateway. It came about when I was presenting my IMPACT model at Reward Gateway's Engagement Excellence Live. I heard Glenn Elliott (CEO and founder of Reward Gateway) speak of the fantastic communications campaigns they had done recently at his company. I was so impressed that

I asked him if he would contribute to the book with a case study. We organized a lunch meeting, and a few weeks later met up so that I could interview him. At the end of the interview he surprised me by offering me a job at his company. So not only did the book (and you) benefit from his examples and case study, but I also got a dream job with a fantastic company. How is that for a happy ending!

INDEX